FIRST CHURCH OF THE BRETHREN

CARLISLE, PA. 17013

What Happens When Women Believe

by

Muriel Larson

© Copyright 1979 by Bible Voice, Inc. All rights re-
served. Printed in U.S.A. Published by Bible Voice,
Inc., P.O. Box 7491, Van Nuys, CA 91409

CONTENTS

This book has been designed for individual reading, but also may be used as a group study course.

Some fictitious names have been used.

FOREWORD

In my Bible teaching and counseling work with women, and through my calling to write the testimonies of God's people, I have heard many thrilling true stories of what happens when women believe.

What happens when women truly believe the precious promises God gives in His Word? Through being filled with hope and faith, they are delivered from depression, emotional and psychosomatic illnesses, unpleasant situations, guilt, fear, worry, and despair. God's promises to help and deliver His people are just as true today as when He inspired holy men of God to write them.

What happens when Christian women believe God for answers when they pray? Jesus said, "Therefore I say unto you, What things soever ye desire, when ye pray, believe that ye receive them, and ye shall have them" (Mark 11:24).

In this book are many true stories of what happened when women believed in various situations. I have included some experiences from my own life, because the Lord has done so many wonderful things for me as I have trusted Him for answers, help, and guidance.

He can do the same for you. Only believe.

Muriel Larson

ABOUT THE AUTHOR:

Muriel Larson—writer, author and composer

More than 2,000 first and reprint rights articles, stories, poems and fillers accepted by about 100 publications, including: *Sunday School Times* and *Gospel Herald, Good News Broadcaster, Grit, National Enquirer, Christian Life Magazine, Moody Monthly, War Cry, The Pentecostal Evangel, Logos Journal, Vital Christianity, Lighted Pathway, Sandlapper, Evangelical Beacon, The Gideon, Opus II, Woman's Touch*, and numerous denominational and interdenominational publishers such as Regular Baptist Press, Scripture Press, Union Gospel Press, Church of God, David C. Cook, Harvest Publications, Wesleyan Publishing House, Free Methodists, Church of the Nazarene, Mennonites, Assemblies of God and many others.

Assignments from Union Gospel Press, Baptist Publications, and Back to the Bible to write Sunday School quarterlies, training union programs, feature columns on the Bible, devotionals for teenagers, and feature stories.

Play produced by WMUU radio station for its "Miracles" program.

Six hymns and four gospel choruses accepted for publication by four publishers.

Served on the faculty of the Western North Carolina Christian Writers' Conference held annually at Black Mountain, N.C.

Listed in Contemporary Authors, Writers' Directory, Personalities of the South, International Who's Who in Community Service, Directory of International Biography, World Who's Who of Authors, and Community Leaders and Noteworthy Americans.

OTHER BOOKS BY MURIEL LARSON:

Baker Book House
DEVOTIONS FOR WOMEN'S GROUPS
HOW TO GIVE A DEVOTION
DEVOTIONS FOR CHILDREN

Warner Press/Pyramid Pub.
LIVING MIRACLES
IT TOOK A MIRACLE

Moody Press
GOD'S FANTASTIC CREATION
THE BIBLE SAYS QUIZ BOOK
JOY EVERY MORNING

Bible Voice/Pillar Books
YOU ARE WHAT YOU THINK

Bible Voice
ARE YOU REAL GOD?
I GIVE UP GOD

Muriel is also a Bible teacher, public speaker, children's evangelist and musician.

1

DISCOVERING TRUE FAITH

*But as many as received him, to them gave he
power to become the sons of God, even to them
that believe on his name.*

John 1:12

"JOY . . . JOY . . . JOY!" the banner at the
front of the church shouted. Patti Lehning looked
at it glumly and couldn't comprehend it. She had
never known any joy at all in her religious experience.

"Sometimes I would come home from my
church crying from emptiness," Patti told me. So
as she looked at that word "JOY," her heart cried
out for it.

Several months after Patti and her family
moved to Greenville, South Carolina, Patti went to
their new church on Easter Sunday. That was when
she saw "JOY" emblazoned across the front of the
sanctuary, along with two other banners. One said
"PEACE" and the other said "LOVE." But Patti
felt cold and lonely.

She looked at the banner that said "PEACE." *Well, it's peaceful here,* she thought. *I'll buy that.* She looked at the one that said, "LOVE." *Surely there must be love in Christianity,* she thought. Then she looked again at the banner that shouted "JOY." *Well, if joy is supposed to be a part of it,* she thought, *that is something I'm missing!*

"Joy, joy," she kept saying to herself. She looked around at the faces of the people in her vicinity. *They don't have joy either,* she thought.

Patti felt an emptiness in her soul as she drove down the highway toward her home. Suddenly she saw a big sign by the side of the road, winking at her with colored flashing lights. "Revival tonight, 7:30," it said. *My, that's a bit unrefined for a church to have a gaudy sign like that!* she thought. But the sign looked so cheerful to her, the thought of it kept coming back to her through the day. A yearning grew in her heart to go to that church that night. Maybe they knew what joy was.

Patti drove to the little church that night and walked in. A great feeling of love hit her as she entered. Sheever seen those people before, nor had they seen her, yet she felt their love engulf her.

When an invitation was given at the end of the service, Patti felt impelled to go forward. She knelt and could hear others by the altar talking to the Lord. *They really know who Jesus is,* she thought, *and He knows them!* Suddenly it dawned on her that Jesus was a real, living Person.

Tears began to flow down Patti's cheeks. "Jesus

is real!" her heart sang. "Jesus is real!"

As Patti stood up, the pastor came to her and introduced himself. After they exchanged a few words, he started praying for her. Suddenly she couldn't stop herself. She began praising the Lord and fell to her knees, tears streaming down her cheeks again.

Joy flooded her soul. Right then she knew Jesus was real and He had died for *her* sins on the cross. No longer was this an abstract fact from a catechism; He was a reality. She knew Him and He knew her. "If there had been a thousand banners shouting 'Joy,'" she told me, "they couldn't have told the joy I felt!"

On her way home Patti said to herself, "I am not going to tell anybody about this experience I've had because no one will believe me." But the minute she walked in the door she couldn't hold it in. "Jesus is real!" she exclaimed to her husband Paul. "Jesus is real!" The next day she had to tell all the neighbors her great discovery.

Patti Lehning had grown up believing what she heard about Jesus in church, but she had never really known Him until that night. That night she believed *on* the Lord Jesus Christ; and the love, peace, and joy imparted by His Spirit became a part of her.

Jesus said, "I am the resurrection and the life; he that believeth in me, though he were dead, yet shall he live" (John 11:25). When Patti trusted in Christ for salvation, He gave her eternal life (John

10:28). Also, according to the Bible, before she knew Him she was "dead in trespasses and sins" (Eph. 2:1). Christ made her truly alive for the first time in her life. No wonder Patti finally knew true joy!

Patti's life was transformed. Although she had never had any musical training, she was inspired by joy and the Holy Spirit to compose 19 gospel songs, all of which were accepted for publication.

Her husband, Paul, was a good man; but Patti suspected he had never yet come to true believing in Christ as his Savior, as she had. She began to pray that he would. About five years after she came to know Christ, Paul did, too. He was also filled with the glorious joy only the Lord can give.

HUNGERING HEARTS

Patti's heart was hungry to really know the Lord and all He had promised to those who truly believe in Him. This heart hunger is the first step toward discovering true faith.

It may begin because someone else is praying for us, that we may be "saved." Saved from what? you may ask. Saved from having to pay the penalty for our sins. The Bible says, "But God commendeth his love toward us, in that, while we were yet sinners, Christ died for us . . . being now justified by his blood, we shall be saved from wrath through him" (Rom. 5:8-9).

We are saved when we realize that Christ died for our sins and accept His sacrifice for us as being personal. "Believe on the Lord Jesus Christ, and thou shalt be saved," the Apostle Paul told the Philippian jailor (Acts 16:31).

Heart hunger for God and His peace and joy may come because we see someone else who has that peace and joy, who has something indefinable and sweet that we would like to have ourselves. This is how God worked in my life.

The Lord sent a young missionary candidate to work with me in the purchasing department at Edison's in West Orange, New Jersey. As I watched Lillian Andreason's sweet, pure, dedicated life, I became convicted about my own self-centered, worldly way of life. As I drank and gambled with my friends, I became disgusted with their filthy jokes and the way they were cheating on their husbands. I wanted to be like Lillian, not like them!

One day when I went in to work I found a tract on my desk. Years later Lillian told me that probably a janitor had put it there. I know now the Lord had led him to do that. As I read that tract, the tears rolled down my cheeks.

"All have sinned and come short of the glory of God," it said; and I knew I had. It said that Jesus Christ had died on the cross for my sins; He had shed His precious blood for me because God loved me. I had known all those things as facts from my childhood, but as I read that tract, the Holy Spirit made them personal realities to me.

I bowed my head right there at the desk and gave my heart to the Lord. I don't remember what

I said. But I remember asking Lillian that afternoon to pray for my husband, that he might come to trust in Christ as I had. For right away I realized how vital it was for everyone to have true heart faith in Christ.

NO ASSURANCE OF SALVATION

I have met and interviewed many women who have "grown up in the church." They had tried to live good lives. Some had taught Sunday school, and one had even become a deaconess. A number of them had gone forward in church at an invitation, they had joined the church, and had been baptized. Or perhaps they had been baptized as babies and had been confirmed at the age of twelve. A number of these, however, had no real assurance of salvation. They felt they had to continually work for it.

This was the way Lynda Weddle believed. She had often asked God for foregiveness for her sins, but she had always arisen from her knees with a feeling of guilt. Even being active in church work didn't help.

One day as Lynda played cards with her friends, they started discussing religion. "Why can't we be sure about going to Heaven?" her friend Shirley asked. "I work so hard in the church, and still I don't know that I'm going to Heaven. I wish I could know!"

"So do I," Lynda said. "I'm always worried that I might do something God wouldn't approve of and I would go to Hell if I died then."

"I must admit it worries me at times when we all get together to play cards," Shirley said. "I was taught when younger it was a sin to play cards. So I keep thinking maybe this will keep me out of Heaven."

Lynda wished she could have helped Shirley; but she couldn't even help herself. She didn't know the answer. How could one be sure of her salvation?

Some of the instruction in their adult Sunday school class began to disturb Lynda and her husband Bill. Instead of being biblical or Christ-centered, discussions revolved around such things as integration, bussing, riots, and other social issues. "Why don't we try another church?" Bill suggested.

They did. There the Word of God was preached; and there Bill went forward to receive Christ as his Savior. Lynda, however, still thought she was already a Christian. It wasn't until she went to a home Bible study that her eyes were opened to the fact that Christ had died for *her*. As the teacher said, "God loves you," Lynda's whole being was filled with joy. "He loves me, He loves me, He loves me!" her heart sang.

"It was just like falling in love," Lynda told me. "Only now I had fallen in love with the Lord who had loved me and given His life for me."

When Lynda came to know the Lord in that personal way, the shackles of salvation by works fell off. She was free—free to really enjoy the Lord, free to rest in His provision for her salvation, free to revel in the abundant life Christ promised those who truly believe in Him.

95% GOOD—100% LOST

I have heard of several great men of God who declared that perhaps 50 percent or more of those who are members of gospel-preaching churches have never truly come to know Christ. I have seen people whom everyone thought sure were born-again Christians come forward in my own church during a revival and confess later they had never truly known Christ before that night.

Mary Gilliam was such a person. One Sunday, however, a message her pastor preached got through to her and the Holy Spirit convicted her. "But you know I am a good person, Lord," she argued. "You will have to let me into Heaven. I have lived such a good life. I have never smoked, drunk, or gone to movies or public swimming beaches. I have never danced or worn makeup. I have been a tither. I have been serving You all these years, and I have even led souls to Christ."

"You are lost. You yourself are lost. You must get right with God," the impression insisted.

Then the words of Jesus sprang into her consciousness: "Not every one that saith unto me, Lord, Lord, shall enter into the kingdom of heaven; but he that doeth the will of my Father which is in heaven. Many will say to me in that day, Lord,

Lord, have we not prophesied in thy name? And in thy name have cast out devils? And in thy name done many wonderful works? And then will I profess unto them, I never knew you; depart from me, ye that work iniquity" (Matt. 7:21-23).

"You can't speak to anyone about this," Mary's pride seemed to say. "You can't go forward and make a fool of yourself. Everyone thinks you are a very good Christian."

All through the years, however, even when she had been leading others to Christ, the Holy Spirit had been dealing with Mary. "Well, good," He had seemed to say, "you know the way of salvation enough to show others to Christ, but how about yourself?" Now the burden became insurmountably heavy. Mary was utterly miserable.

One night Mary received a phone call from her oldest son, Joe, who, as a junior at a Christian university, was preparing for the ministry. "Mom, guess what?" he exclaimed. "I just got saved!"

Mary listened in amazement as her son told her how the burden on his heart had been lifted. When she went to church the following Sunday, the message and the Holy Spirit spoke strongly to her. "This is the last time I'm going to speak to your heart," the Holy Spirit seemed to say. "This is your last chance to be saved. You are lost, and you are on your way to Hell."

Suddenly the full realization that she was a sinner dawned on her. Because she had always lived what she thought was a good life, she had never seen that she was a sinner who came short of the glory of God. For the first time in her life Mary saw that Christ had died for *her* sins.

Before the pastor could even give an altar call, Mary was on her feet and down the aisle. "Save me, Lord," she cried softly, as she fell to her knees. "I believe You died for my sins!"

A great mountain was lifted from her heart that day. "What a wonderful relief it was!" she told me, her eyes sparkling. "As I walked out of that prayer room, I knew I was a child of God. At the age of 47 I had been born again!"

THROUGH A MAZE

Although God's plan of salvation is so simple that even a child can understand it and be saved, many people seem to stumble over its very simplicity. Like Cain, they feel they must do something to earn their salvation.

My friend, Jean Westfall, about whom I wrote the book, *Are You Real, God?*, thought the answer lay in baptism and church membership. In fact, she was baptized twice by sprinkling and three times by immersion in churches of four denominations. In none of this did she find peace.

Because of personal experiences, as well as because of what she saw in the lives of other professing Christians, Jean became cynical concerning religion. She began to study the teachings of philosophers and psychology, hoping to find the answers to life somewhere in them. Even though she found what she thought were some good ideas, she still had no peace. She kept her stereo going day and night to drown out her thoughts.

Jean and her friends in her Atlanta apartment complex held many Saturday night parties. Early in the morning the parties often ended with everyone sitting in a circle discussing God, His existence, and the meaning of life. Jean finally decided that Altizer's "God-is-dead" theory best fit in with her experience in life. She began thinking of herself as an atheist.

Then God opened the door for Jean to go to work for a Christian dentist as a dental technician. She noticed right away there was something different about Mike Hopping. He told her about how Jesus Christ had transformed his life and his wife's, how they had finally come to know true love, peace, and joy. Jean yearned to have what the Hoppings had.

Before Jean went on vacation that summer, Mike gave her a booklet called "The Ministry of the Holy Spirit," by Bill Bright. As she read that booklet, while curled up on a sofa in her parents' farmhouse in West Virginia, Jean saw it contained God's plan of salvation. *I know all this*, she thought impatiently.

Then she read a statement that stopped her. "If you have never committed your intellect and your will and your emotions to Christ, you cannot have a personal relationship to Him." She was startled. She couldn't bear sitting on the sofa any longer.

Jumping up, she walked outside and strolled through the farmyard and out into a field.

As she thought over her life and some things her father and the Hoppings had said to her, she suddenly realized something. *Salvation is not a matter of my being baptized or keeping certain rules people make up or anything I can say or do. It's a matter of my turning my will and my life over to Christ!*

Looking up at the blue sky, she said, "God, if You are who You say You are, and if Your Son is real, I invite Him into my heart right now!" She felt so sorry for all the sins she had committed, and, with her whole heart, turned from her old way of life to God's way in that moment.

Suddenly everything looked very beautiful to her. The burden on her heart lifted and she knew a peace and joy she had never known before. Jean's life was transformed when she came to the Lord humbly, as a little child. Her search for truth and peace was ended. She has been serving the Lord ever since.

Candi Long also went through a maze to find the Lord. During her college years she alternately rejected God and searched for the truth. When a woman testified at Candi's school how Christ had delivered her from alcoholism, had transformed her life, and had given her peace and joy, Candi was glad for her, but felt slightly envious. It didn't occur to her that she could have what that woman had.

Candi went on to graduate school at the University of Georgia. There she became friends with a medium, who interested her in spiritualism. Candi began to read books about spiritualism, Jeanne Dixon, Edgar Cayce, and others. She started taking a course in metaphysics at a spiritualist community near her home in Florida. But the immoral life her medium friend led turned her off, and put doubts in her mind concerning this way.

At an engagement party Candi attended one night, two friends told her about the wonderful new life they had found in Christ and explained God's way of salvation to her. They gave her a booklet to read.

As she read the booklet in her room later that night, God's way suddenly became clear to her. She bowed her head and received Christ as her Savior. Peace filled her heart, and she knew she had found what she had been seeking. Candi went into the full-time service of the Lord and has played musical instruments and sung to His glory from one end of the country to the other.

SIMPLY BELIEVE

There is no need to go through a tortuous maze to come to faith in Christ, to know His love, peace, and joy. The Bible says, "So then faith cometh by hearing, and hearing by the word of God" (Rom. 10:17). The Holy Spirit uses the Word of God, which is "powerful and sharper than any two-edged sword," to show us the truth about ourselves and about Christ. All we need to do is to believe it and accept it.

SOMETHING YOU CAN DO:

1. Read John 3:1-21, 35-36. Before reading, ask the Lord to open your eyes to the truth.

2. If you have any doubt as to whether you have been born again through faith in Christ, call on Him right now to save you. "Whosoever shall call upon the name of the Lord shall be saved" (Rom. 10:13).

3. For study or discussion:

(a) How does a person become a Christian? (See Romans 3:23, 6:23, 5:8, 10:9-10, 13; Ephesians 2:8-9; Titus 3:5-7; Revelation 3:20.)

(b) Why is it vital for a person to believe *on* the Lord Jesus Christ? (See John 3:36, 8:21, 14:6, 20:31; Romans 1:16, 8:1-3; Hebrews 9:27-28.)

2

TRANSFORMED LIVES

Put on the new self, created to be like God in true righteousness and holiness

—Eph. 4:24, (NIV)

"What about people who make a decision for Christ and there is no evidence in their lives that they are Christians?" I have often been asked that question. It poses quite a problem for many people, both Christians and non-Christians. Some stumble over it. Others use it as an excuse for backsliding or for not coming to church. But there are answers to that question.

One answer is that many people "make a decision" or go forward to join the church and get baptized, but they have not repented of their sins or given their hearts to Christ. They have not believed in their hearts in the living Christ (Rom. 10:9). They have not been born again by the Holy Spirit. They never became real Christians, even though they may have joined the church and decided to "turn over a new leaf." That is not salvation.

Another answer is that some who come to Christ do show evidence of a change after their conversion, even as probably the Corinthian Christians did. But by the time the Apostle Paul wrote his letters to those Corinthians, they were a sorry lot! They were divisive, factious, clannish, prideful, and disorganized. They sued one another (1 Cor. 6), and some were living immorally (1 Cor. 5-6).

Why was this? Paul said they were still carnal, still babes in Christ (1 Cor. 3:1-4). They had not grown as Christians. If a baby doesn't grow, he is something pitiful. Even so is a Christian who doesn't grow. Paul advised the Corinthians to check and make sure if they were really Christians and not just pretending (cf. 2 Cor. 13:5, LB).

There is good reason to doubt the faith of a person in whom there has been no real lasting change. To those same Corinthians Paul wrote, "Therefore if anyone is in Christ, he is a new creation; the old has gone, the new has come!" (2 Cor. 5:17, NIV). In both my personal work for the Lord and my writing work I have seen the reality of this great truth.

In my own life also it has been very true. After I surrendered to the Lord at the age of 24 I had new desires. I quit my card club; I no longer wanted to run with that crowd. I started going to church, reading my Bible, and seeking to reach my husband for Christ. Over a period of several years the Holy Spirit worked on me to take one un-Christian thing after another out of my life; and He has continued to work on me through the years concerning anything in me that is not Christlike.

This is a great truth: when a woman truly believes on Jesus Christ for salvation, the Spirit of God comes to dwell in her body (1 Cor. 6:19, 2 Cor. 6:16). A woman with God's Spirit living in her cannot be comfortable when sinning. She may quench the Spirit, may try to drown out His quiet voice with activity and sound. But she cannot get away from Him.

The Bible says concerning a person who has been truly born of the Spirit, "Being confident of this very thing, that he which hath begun a good work in you will perform it until the day of Jesus Christ" (Phil. 1:6). It is God's plan to conform every one of His children to the image of His Son (Rom. 8:29).

· THE WORST CHARACTER

When I lived in North Plainfield, New Jersey, I went on Sunday afternoons to the Elizabeth County Jail to hold a service for the women. As Millie Brown and I walked in one Sunday the matron said apprehensively to us, "I hope you don't have any trouble with that Marie. She's a tough one—the worst character we have had in here for a long time. I doubt if you can do anything with her!"

About a dozen women awaited us. After we sang several old favorite hymns, I brought a salvation message, about how Jesus had come to set the prisoners free. The women listened intently. When I gave an invitation to receive Christ, four of them raised their hands. They bowed their heads and prayed with me a prayer of repentance for sins and acceptance of Christ as their Savior.

Promising to pray for the women and to leave Gospels of John for them, I wrote down their names. One of them was Marie.

"Please write to me, will you?" she pleaded. "My trial comes up this week, and I probably won't be here the next time you come. I'd like to keep in touch with you." As I left, I wondered, *Will Christ make a difference in Marie's life?*

The following week the matron said to us, "I don't know what you people did to that Marie who was here last week, but she became a completely different person—cooperative and pleasant!"

Two months after I wrote my first letter to Marie, I received one from her. "I know you'll be glad to hear that I have been made the 'Honor Girl' of my cottage," she wrote. "Jesus has given me back my husband and two little girls. They will be waiting for me when I get out."

Christ does change lives. And when women truly believe in Him and believe that with God nothing is impossible, their prayers are answered. Jesus said to His followers, "If ye shall ask anything in my name, I will do it" (John 14:14).

FROM MISERY TO JOY

Tempe Brown came to the place in her life where she had everything she had always thought she wanted: money, popularity, a new expensive house. But she was miserable.

Tempe's singing career had blossomed as she had moved up the entertainment ladder to sing in all the top nightclubs in Oklahoma City at one time or another. During the day Tempe worked as editor of *Key* magazine. "I became acquainted with just about everyone who was anybody in that city," she told me.

Tempe had three children by her first husband, from whom she had been divorced. Because she was seldom able to be home in her striving to make a living, her two daughters got in with a bad crowd and went astray. Tempe was heartsick when they were sent to a girls' reformatory. Although she was a success in the entertainment and business worlds, she felt she had failed as a mother. Now she sang her blues songs with even more feeling. She also drank more than ever before.

One night, just before Tempe had to leave for the nightclub, she received a phone call from her brother Don about another brother. "Jim is in the hospital," he said, "and he is very ill."

"What's wrong?"

"Leukemia," he answered, "and we all know how serious that can be. Pray!"

Tempe came home that night in a drunken stupor, just as she had many other nights. *I wonder if*

God answers a drunk's prayers? she pondered. But she looked up and pleaded, "Please don't let Jim die, God. He's a fine man. Take me instead. I'm not much good!"

The next thing she heard about Jim amazed her. All his symptoms had disappeared. His doctors were astonished and they couldn't understand how it had happened. Tempe's mother told her over the phone, "Jim says he has found the Lord and God has healed him. He seems like a new man!" Thrilled, Tempe wondered what had happened.

One night she ran into a pianist she knew named Harlan Rogers. "What's this I hear about you and your band, Harlan?" she asked. "You fellows used to be freaked out on drugs, and now I understand you're freaked out on religion!"

"That's right, Tempe," Harlan answered, "only it's not religion—it's Jesus! We all came to know Jesus Christ as our Savior."

Not everything Harlan said to her registered that night. All she could remember was that as he kept talking about "my Jesus" this and "my Jesus" that, his face had a happy glow, as if he had swallowed a light bulb.

When she got back to her apartment, she sat on her bed and said, "OK, God. What's so important about Jesus? If He is all that important, I want to know what the deal is!" Several days later she received a Christian book from her brother Jim, which at his suggestion she started to read daily.

Her eyes began to be opened.

Later, Tempe's parents sent her a copy of Charles Colson's book, *Born Again*. As she read it, she wept. "I saw myself as a lost sinner, unable to do anything to help myself," she told me. "When I finished reading the book, I bowed my head and asked Jesus to be my Savior. I had seen what Jesus had done for Jim, for Harlan Rogers, for Charles Colson. I wanted Him to do it for me—and He did!"

The Lord led Tempe to give up the rock band she had formed, and then led her to an old friend, who turned out to be a dedicated Christian. With this friend's help Tempe began to grow in her new life as a Christian. With the Lord's help she kicked her bad habits of drinking and smoking.

Now Tempe is living and singing for Jesus Christ. Her life has been transformed. Her son has also come to know Christ.

Yes, Christ does change lives. From a miserable existence where she had everything the world has to offer, my friend Tempe Brown has graduated to the infinitely higher plane where she has everything the Lord has to offer: peace, joy, and the abundant life.

WOMEN AGLOW

Sometimes you can tell at a glance that a person is a Christian. As Tempe said, they look like they have swallowed a light bulb. Something shines out of their eyes, their faces. It is the light of Christ.

Although we may not see this evidence in many of the professing Christians we encounter, it is actually Christ's "norm" for His followers. "Ye are the light of the world," He said (Matt. 5:14). "Be filled with the Spirit," the Bible says (Eph. 5:18). When you are filled with the Spirit of Christ, others see Christ and His light in you. He is "Christ in you, the hope of glory" (Col. 1:27).

Bonnie, a teenager I became acquainted with who had indulged in drugs and sex since she was 12, told me how she walked into a Christian bookstore one day to buy a book about coffeehouses. She planned to do a term paper for her psychology class at Greenville TEC.

The young woman who waited on her was about her age, 18 or 19. Tamra Wilson began talking to Bonnie enthusiastically about Jesus and what He had done for her. *She's crazy*, Bonnie thought, as she noticed the gleam in the other girl's eyes. *A religious fanatic!*

As she stared at the other girl and listened to her, however, Bonnie got the definite impression that this girl had something she didn't have. She seemed so pure and radiant that suddenly Bonnie felt dirty inside. She hated the other girl for that. Furious, she walked out of the store without the book she had paid for.

She returned to the store. There that girl was, with her big smile and shining eyes. "I had never seen anyone look so happy and contented," Bonnie told me. Tamra put her hand on Bonnie's book and started talking again. She told Bonnie about two coffeehouses that were in Greenville where she could go for further information.

Bonnie went to see the director of one of the coffeehouses several days later. She noticed he also had something different about him; he also talked to her about Jesus. During the week that followed Bonnie was in a turmoil. She knew she was a lost sinner; she had gone about as deep into sin as any girl could go. She was 18, addicted to drugs, jaded.

An urgent desire to talk to that unusual girl again drove Bonnie back to the bookstore. This time, however, as Tamra talked about Jesus to her, she found herself actually liking this radiant young woman.

After visiting the coffeehouses several times, one night Bonnie prayed with a Christian girl to receive Christ as her Savior. Washed clean, Bonnie no longer needed dope to help her forget how sordid her life had been. She had found deliverance because she had seen the light of Christ in some of His disciples.

The Bible tells Christians, "You are to live clean, innocent lives as children of God in a dark world full of people who are crooked and stubborn. Shine out among them like beacon lights" (Phil. 2:15, LB).

Christ, the transformer, fills women who truly believe with the mighty power of His Spirit and causes them to radiate His light for God's glory.

SOMETHING YOU CAN DO:

1. Read Ephesians 4:17-32. Before reading, ask the Lord to open your eyes to what advice He has for you in this Scripture.

2. If you are a Christian, and you haven't been living a good, holy life for your Lord, why not kneel and fully yield yourself to His control? Make Him really your Lord. Become a light for Jesus.

3. For study or discussion:

(a) What principles should govern a Christian's life and behavior? (See Romans 12:2; 1 Corinthians 6:12b, 19-20, 8:13, 10:23, 31; 2 Corinthians 10:8; Colossians 3:17; 1 Thessalonians 5:22; 1 John 2:15-17.)

(b) How does a Christian become a light and testimony for the Lord? (See Matthew 5:16; John 15:5-12; Romans 13:8-14; Philippians 1:21, 2:2-5, 14-16; 4:4-8; Colossians 3:1-23.)

3

DELIVERANCE FROM SLAVERY

But thanks be to God that, though you used to be slaves to sin, you wholeheartedly obeyed the form of teaching to which you were committed. You have been set free from sin and have become slaves to righteousness.

Romans 6:17-18, (NIV)

According to God's Word, all those who have not yet come to true belief in Jesus Christ as their Savior are slaves to sin. "We know that the law is spiritual," Paul wrote to the Romans, "but I am unspiritual, sold as a slave to sin. I do not know what I am doing. For what I want to do I do not do, but what I hate I do" (7:14-15, NIV).

Paul may have been describing how he was before he became a Christian, or how he was when he was young in the Lord. But he was not that way when he wrote the Book of Romans. He ended chapter seven by exclaiming, "What a wretched man I am! Who will rescue me from this body of death? Thanks be to God—through Jesus Christ our Lord!" (Romans 7:24-25, NIV).

The key word in chapter seven of Romans is "I." Notice how often Paul uses that little self-centered word. But he goes from that depressing state of slavery into chapter eight, where the whole theme is different. It is a theme of victory. And who is the Person on whom the emphasis is put in this chapter? It is God. In fact, the Godhead is given the pre-eminence in this chapter: God the Father, God the Son, and God the Holy Spirit. The key word in Romans 8 is "Spirit."

Chapter seven reveals the defeat suffered by those who live in the flesh, where "I" predominates. Chapter eight reveals the victory possible to those who live in the spirit, who are led by the Spirit of God and who by His power put to death the misdeeds of their bodies.

Many people down through the ages have found instant deliverance from the sins that had enslaved them, when they have trusted Jesus Christ as their Savior. I have interviewed numerous people who told me that on the very day they gave their hearts to Christ they were able to throw away their drugs, liquor, cigarettes, or whatever they were enslaved to. Through faith in Christ and the power of the Holy Spirit, prostitutes, alcoholics, and drug addicts have become women of God.

DELIVERANCE FROM DRUGS

When I met Sandra, she was a radiant Christian, aglow with love for her Savior. She had good reason to feel that way toward Him. He had rescued her from a life that was worse than death.

Before Sandra had trusted in Christ, she had overdosed on heroin and other drugs five times. She had been a heroin addict for four years and had a habit that cost her close to $100 every day.

Sandra had looked forward to marrying her high school sweetheart. But eventually, wanted for armed robbery and murder, he made the FBI's 10 most-wanted list. When he was caught, he was sentenced to 99 years in state prison. Sandra's dreams went down the drain.

After another disappointing love affair, Sandra tried to commit suicide several times, and overdosed on heroin five times. Miraculously, her life was spared, but her heroin habit had grown to that $100-a-day stage. Sandra began to realize she couldn't go on the way she was. When she learned about a Christian drug rehabilitation center, she admitted herself to its care. "Cold turkey," the director told her.

"People die that way," Sandra protested. But she didn't die. And during the days that followed she saw that the people at the center had a peace, joy, and love for people she had never witnessed before. Finally one Sunday night at church Sandy walked down to the altar weeping. She had suddenly realized that Christ, the Son of God, had died for her sins; and she believed. Humbly she asked Him to forgive her and come into her life. He did.

Sandra was delivered from addiction to heroin and cigarettes. Her life was transformed. She was so happy she wanted to tell everyone about Christ, and she did. Before long, her brother, her parents, and a former drug pusher friend of hers also came to Christ. Sandra became a worker with the center. Today she is still in the Lord's full-time service with the dedicated Christian husband the Lord gave her.

Christ changes lives. Christ gives those who believe in Him a brand new start. Christ delivers us from slavery to sin when we yield completely to Him and seek continually to be filled with His Spirit, when we truly believe that He is able to give us "the victory that overcometh the world" (1 John 5:4).

DELIVERANCE FROM ALCOHOL

Edith was an alcoholic. She worked as a housekeeper for a family in Corpus Christi, Texas; and her employer periodically threatened to fire her because she was so often in a drunken stupor.

"Every day she searched my room, but she never found where I hid my liquor," Edith told me. "You will not find a more sneaky person than a drunkard. I hid it in the largest jar I could find, put flowers in it, and set it right out on the table. I drank gin, even though I didn't like it, because it couldn't be so easily detected by smell. I was a great mouthwash customer!"

Her employer's 80-year-old mother came to visit, and Edith was asked to take the elderly woman to church that Sunday. Even after the elderly woman left, Edith was drawn back to that church week after week. After attending for two months, one Sunday morning when Edith awoke a thought came to her: "*All right now, what do you want? Do you want to go to church, or do you want to keep on drinking? You can't have it both ways.*"

"*Well, do I want to continue living?*" Edith asked herself. All of a sudden a wonderful realization struck her: *I haven't thought about wanting to die lately*! Edith had been miserable for so long. She had hardly been able to stand herself because of her drunkenness, her addiction to alcohol. So she decided to stop drinking. "I tried real hard," she told me, "but I couldn't stop. I was too far gone."

She finally went to the pastor of the church and said, "I would like to stop drinking, but I can't."

At first the pastor talked to Edith about her need for salvation. But she didn't quite comprehend what he said and kept insisting that what she wanted was deliverance from her drink problem. "OK," he said, "let's pray."

"I had been an alcoholic for many years, but from that day on I never touched a drop!" Edith told me. "It was nothing but the power of God."

During the month that followed that prayer, however, Edith found it hard going because she still had a desire for alcohol. When the pastor asked her how she was doing, she told him about her problem. "Well, let's pray again," he said. "The Lord knows you don't want to drink." He laid hands on Edith and prayed that the Lord would take away the desire for alcohol.

"From that day on I did not want to drink," Edith testifies. "God took away even the desire for it."

Edith still had not received Jesus Christ as her Savior. But God works in the hearts of people in all different ways. He knew that because of Edith's turmoil-filled past life she needed love and softening. One day Edith asked the minister, "What do I have to do to join the church?"

"You have to accept Jesus Christ as your personal Savior," he said. "Do you accept Him as your personal Savior? Do you believe He is the Son of God and died for your sins on the cross?"

"Yes," Edith answered. "Yes, I do accept Him. I do believe!" For it suddenly dawned on her—*If I couldn't stop drinking, then who made me stop? No human being did that for me. God did it! He's got to be mighty great and powerful. He must really care for me to do that! So then maybe I can also trust Him and commit my life to Him.*

When she had studied the catechism in Germany as she was growing up, Edith had learned that Jesus Christ had died on the cross for sinners. Now she knew He was still alive and He cared for her. Now she saw Him as her personal Savior. She followed her pastor in prayer to receive Him into her heart that day.

In Edith's case God delivered her from bondage to alcohol in order to bring her to belief in Christ. From my experience in playing musical instruments, singing, and testifying in rescue missions all over the United States, I know that a number of those who make professions of faith in Christ may go back to alcohol after a period of abstinence. Edith's coming to true faith in Christ and having His Spirit come to dwell in her heart was absolutely essential to her continued deliverance from alcohol. She told me how the Lord's hand was on her during the months and years following her conversion, to keep her from returning to the bottle.

The Bible warns us, "Be self-controlled and alert. Your enemy the devil prowls around like a roaring lion looking for someone to devour. Resist him, standing firm in the faith . . ." (1 Pet. 5:8-9, NIV).

The Christian woman who has been delivered from alcohol or drugs must seek to walk close to the Lord for the rest of her life. She must look to Him in faith believing that He can keep her on the straight and narrow path. Christianity is a way of life, and we find the rules for walking that way in God's Word. That's why it is so important for us to keep reading it, day by day; it buoys us up in our faith and in our knowledge of the way He wants us to go.

DELIVERANCE FROM CIGARETTES

I realize that some Christians think it is all right to smoke. But the truth is that smoking is not only an enslaving costly habit, but it is very harmful to a person's body. A Christian's body is the temple of God and is not to be defiled. It is holy (1 Cor. 3:17).

Bea Fishter came to know Christ when she was about 36 years old, and she had accumulated some bad habits by that time. She and her husband Bob had liked to hang out in barrooms and drink, until they got saved. The Lord took them out of that way of life immediately. They threw out the beer in their refrigerator. The church became the place they most loved to go. They were there every time the doors were open. I met Bea at that church, and she and I became the best of friends.

Bea also had had quite a bad temper. She told me that once she actually tried to stab her husband with a knife in a fit of anger, before they had become Christians. The Lord delivered her from that temper, too.

But Bea and Bob were still smoking cigarettes when we met them, and Bea was really addicted. She had two teenagers at that time. "We had the young people at our house last night," she told me one day, "and it really hit me what a bad example I would be to them with my smoking. But I have been smoking for so long I don't know how I can give it up."

"Don't you believe the Lord can deliver you

from that addiction?" I asked. "He doesn't want His children to be slaves to anything that destroys their bodies. Let's pray about it." So we prayed.

The following Wednesday night a guest speaker brought the message at prayer meeting. It dealt with how a Christian could overcome bad habits. The speaker gave an illustration of someone who held a little bird in his hand, opened up the hand, and the bird flew away. "You need to open up your hand and let God take that habit away," he said.

That's just what I need to do, Bea thought. *I've been thinking I had to overcome my smoking habit. But if I believe in God's power, He will take it away, if I just open up my hand and let go of it!*

When she went home that night, she told Bob of her decision to give up smoking. "Oh, that's not hard to do," he laughed. "I'll give it up, too."

Bob seemed to have no trouble at all in giving up the habit. But during that first week without cigarettes Bea was so sick from withdrawal that she had to go to bed for several days. "I know if I just keep looking to the Lord, He will bring me through this!" she told me. And He did. By the end of the week she recovered and felt much better.

Bea never smoked another cigarette. She went on to become an outstanding soulwinner and worker with children, one of the most beautiful lights for Jesus I have ever known.

It has saddened me to see how many Christians

have allowed one little habit like smoking to keep them from becoming the testimony and servants of Christ they could. It's sad to see Christian women destroying their bodies with cancer or heart disease because of this enslaving habit. If a Christian woman will really believe that "with God nothing is impossible," she can throw the things away and have victory. Victory doesn't depend on us; it depends on God who has the power over all things. All we have to do is believe.

DELIVERANCE STEP BY STEP

"Have patience with me—God isn't done with me yet!" Have you ever heard this saying? Well, it is true of all of us, isn't it? Usually when we first come to Christ, He takes the obvious sins out of our lives. But as we go along, looking to Him and wanting to please Him, we find the Holy Spirit convicting us of this way we talk or that thing we do that really isn't loving or Christlike. The closer we draw to the Lord, the more sensitive we become to the pleading and conviction of the Holy Spirit about shortcomings in our lives.

Through the years of our lives all kinds of things and people influence us. We might find, for instance, that we have fallen into the habit of verbally tearing other Christians apart, criticizing and complaining. That one goes clear back to the Israelites, who offended God with their murmuring and rebellion against Moses.

For some time I was in close contact with some

people who had that habit. I started becoming critical and unloving toward my fellow Christians myself. The Holy Spirit drew me up short as I read God's Word. "By this shall all men know that ye are my disciples, if ye have love one to another," Jesus said (John 13:35).

As I repented of my sin and sought the Lord's help in overcoming it, I began to have the victory. One of the hardest things to overcome is the mouth! But believe this: with God nothing is impossible. He can put such a loving spirit in our hearts for others that it overcomes a critical, condemnatory spirit.

What is the greatest commandment? Jesus said it was two-fold: to love God and love our neighbor. Therefore I think the greatest sin we can commit is to break that twin command. It is worse by far than drinking, smoking, or any other such fleshly habit. Yet how many of us who profess Christ break that command in one way or another! Christ's Spirit gives us the power to truly love, even as He loves.

Before Vivian Weller became a Christian, she drank heavily and was addicted to drugs. Through the love that Christians showed her, however, she came to know Christ as her Savior. She became a "new creature in Christ."

Her victory over the drinking and drugs came right away. Some months later she prayed and asked deliverance from cigarettes, and God gave it. One remarkable victory the Lord gave Vivian as she leaned on Him was victory over a phobia she had. She had been in a number of car accidents before she was saved and was afraid to drive in traffic. But as she stepped out in faith and believed the Lord for deliverance from this fear—so that she could drive to church when her husband was out of town—God gave her the victory in even that.

VICTORY OVER ANYTHING

God doesn't want His children to be slaves to anything. Do you believe that? Whatever we are slaves to in this world, that is our god; we cannot perfectly be God's servants and do His will. Therefore it is His will for us to be delivered from any kind of slavery.

How do we get the victory?

Number One: Believe that with God all things are possible. Believe that with His help you can have the victory.

Number Two: Run to God and submit yourself to Him whenever you are tempted, the Bible says. Then you will be able to resist the devil in the power of God and he will flee from you (James 4:7-8).

Number Three: Use the method our Lord Jesus Christ used to resist Satan and temptation (Matt. 4:1-11). Jesus met every temptation from the devil with a verse of Scripture. Memorize appropriate Scripture verses so that you are ready when tempted by some besetting sin. Believe in the power of God's Word to rout temptation.

When you pray and ask God for help, believe that He will give it. Believe He will deliver you. Jesus said, "What things soever ye desire, when ye pray, believe that ye receive them, and ye shall have them" (Mark 11:24). Women who believe get their prayers answered.

SOMETHING YOU CAN DO:

1. Read Romans 6:1-14. Before reading, ask the Lord for understanding.

2. Are you a slave to food, drink, drugs, cigarettes, or anything else? Memorize Romans 13:14—"But put ye on the Lord Jesus Christ, and make not provision for the flesh, to fulfill the lusts thereof." Also memorize First Corinthians 3:17 and 10:13, Philippians 3:19 and 4:13, and the Scripture listed below. Tempted by sexual sin? Memorize First Thessalonians 4:3-4, 7.

3. For study or discussion:

(a) How can a person overcome an enslaving habit? (See Romans 12:1-2; 1 Corinthians 6:12b, 19-20, 10:23, 31; Ephesians 6:10-18; Colossians 3:2-3, 17; 1 Thessalonians 5:22; Hebrews 2:18; and 1 John 2:15-17.)

(b) What habits might be considered sinful for a Christian? Why?

4

DELIVERANCE FROM DESPAIR

Cast thy burden upon the Lord, and he shall sustain thee: he shall never suffer the righteous to be moved.

Psalm 55:22

Do you feel as if you are at the end of your rope—that you just can't stand anymore as far as the situation you are in? I've been there. I've known what it was to feel in the depths of despair. But would you believe that it is a stepping stone for the child of God to grow in grace and become strong in the Lord?

It all depends on what you do, how you meet such a life situation. You may cry day and night; you may take to the bottle and try to drown your woe; you may become bitter and complain to everyone you meet. Or you may throw yourself completely on the Lord. When you do that, then you discover what the Bible speaks of when it says we can have the "peace of God which passeth all understanding" (Phil. 4:7). This can only be had, however, through our having the full belief that God is going to work things out for us in the best way possible (Romans 8:28), that He is our rock, our fortress, and our deliverer, as the psalmist said (Psalm 18:2).

DESPAIR OVER PHYSICAL HANDICAP

Even dedicated Christians sometimes go through the deep valley of despair. Bea Fishter went through that valley when her left knee disintegrated from rheumatoid arthritis and she had to start wearing a full leg brace. "I won't be able to do anything wearing this brace!" she exclaimed despondently to her husband Bob.

"But you don't want to be bedridden or tied to your wheelchair, do you?" Bob asked. "That's the only alternative. Come on, Bea, don't be discouraged. It isn't like you to give up easily. You can do it!"

Throughout Bea's illness, during the various times she had been in the hospital because of her affliction, Bob had been a source of encouragement and strength to her. Bea had also kept looking to the Lord and He had sustained her. But now Bea was in a slough of despond she couldn't seem to get out of. When she went to see her Christian doctor, she cried rebelliously, "I don't want to be tied up in this old brace!"

Dr. Robert Barnes looked at her curiously. "Bea Fishter, this isn't like you. You have always been full of joy. What has happened to your faith?"

"I just don't want this old thing on my leg!" she wailed. "And I'm so miserable, I'm not fit to live with these days!"

Sympathizing with her, the doctor prescribed tranquillizers; but after taking only a few, Bea found she didn't need them anymore.

"I had friends praying for me," she told me when I visited her in New Jersey about six months later. "And what Dr. Barnes said bothered me. I read Second Corinthians 12:9 and suddenly I realized I was rebelling against the Lord. That's why I didn't have His joy in my heart and wasn't a testimony for Him. I bowed my head in prayer and accepted the leg brace as from His hand. I was no longer miserable, but happy again. I put away the tranquillizers."

While going through this testing of her faith, Bea almost gave up her service for the Lord. "I just can't work in Children's Church anymore," she told her pastor's wife, Alice.

"I know you've had a lot of pain and can't get around as you used to, Bea," Alice answered. "But the children love you, and you're so good with them! Perhaps you can continue conducting the meeting while sitting in a chair."

"Oh, no!" Bea exclaimed. "A leader of little children has to be able to do what *they* do—to march around with them and do all the motions. If you're telling a story about Zacchaeus, you've got to be Zacchaeus. No, Alice, you know my heart is in this work, but they need someone else to do it."

"Well, suppose we let others be your arms and legs, Bea, and you be in charge of the whole operation?" suggested Alice. "We don't want to lose your know-how. This way you can pass it on to others."

Thus, through Bea Fishter's handicap, dependability, and faith, was born a unique training program at New Durham Chapel in Piscataway, New Jersey, which prepared many young and new Christians to serve the Lord.

"Our Children's Church program is giving a number of young people and new Christians an opportunity to serve the Lord," Bea told me. "It is also good experience and training for them. We have eight pianists and eight leaders and a number of helpers. Each worker has a turn every month. We take pianists, storytellers, and handcraft helpers from seventh grade up; but the leaders are either adults or older young people."

Bea prepared the material, planned the programs and handwork, and assigned the workers. Every Sunday she was there to make sure all the workers had come. They seldom let someone as faithful as Bea Fishter down!

Bea had to give up the work when her physical condition became so bad that her husband had to bring her to church on a stretcher. But her radiant faith, peace, and joy in the Lord were a testimony to the entire church, as well as to those to whom she always witnessed in the hospital. When Bea went to be with the Lord, everyone knew it was graduation day for her.

DESPAIR ABOUT OVERWHELMING PROBLEMS

Another person who went through the vale of despair was Deane Heath of Greenville, South Carolina. Deane was suddenly faced with a terrible problem. How does a woman tell a heart patient who loves her that she might have cancer? Dean was more concerned for her husband than she was for herself. She loved Dick dearly. What would happen when he heard the news?

"How can I tell him, Lord?" she cried silently, clutching the steering wheel of her car. "It might kill him!"

Dick had had a serious heart attack just six weeks before. When he was discharged from the hospital the doctor had warned Deane, "Dick must not be excited or upset in any way. It could be fatal to him."

Then several weeks later Deane had discovered the lump in her breast. After her doctor examined her, he looked worried. "What's wrong?" she asked.

"You either have an abscess," he answered, "or you have something in there that has to come out in a hurry!"

On Wednesday Deane went for the tests the doctor had ordered. After looking at the results the technician excused herself saying, "I want to let the doctor see this." When Deane left the hospital that day she knew from the way the technician and doctor had acted that she had a malignancy. She cried all the way home. Before going into the house to face Dick, she sat in her car praying to the Lord for strength and wisdom. When she went in, she just told Dick she would have to have surgery.

Then the phone rang and her son called her. "Mom, it's the doctor and he wants to speak to you."

Moving to the phone as if in a dream, she picked it up. "You'll have to have surgery right away," the doctor said.

"Is it malignant?" she asked.

"I don't know," he answered, "but I don't like what I see."

When she asked him how long she should plan to be in the hospital, he answered, "Three weeks." She felt suddenly weak inside, as if she were about to collapse. Dick was standing right behind her.

"What did he say?" he asked.

"I've got to have surgery," she whispered, tears flowing down her cheeks.

Dick sat down heavily, just staring without a word. He seemed to be in a state of shock. "Oh, Lord," Deane prayed, "please don't let him have another heart attack!"

That night Dick took the sleeping pills that had been prescribed for him. But Deane lay in bed wide awake and full of despair. "What shall I do with my husband, Lord?" she asked. "What about my young son? Who is going to look after them while I'm in the hospital? And oh, Lord, I've worked so hard in my beauty salon for so many years to help Dick, Jr., through college and medical school! Next year he will finally become a doctor. Will we live to see it?"

Another thought struck her. Perhaps the Lord was punishing her for something she had done or failed to do. "Lord, you don't spank a child without letting him know why!" she cried silently. "Speak to my heart. Tell me why!"

She thought over her life. She had faithfully taught the Women's Sunday School class at her church and had often witnessed for the Lord. She had tried to the best of her ability to live a dedicated life for Christ. She couldn't think of anything that stood between her and the Lord.

The longer she lay there the more distraught she became. *I'll end up in a mental hospital if I go on like this*, she thought wildly. She felt so helpless.

"Lord, help me!" she pleaded, finally throwing herself completely on him. Then His strength filled her being. Perfect peace calmed her heart.

For the first time Romans 8:28 became personal to her: "And we know that *all* things work together for good to them that love God, to them who are the called according to his purpose." Deane loved God with all her heart. She knew all this would work together for good for herself and her family. She turned all her problems over to the Lord and went to sleep.

The next day her older son and his wife flew up from Charleston and her mother-in-law came to take care of her husband and younger son. She went to the hospital for surgery.

The lump was malignant, a fast-growing cancer. Radical surgery had to be performed, but Deane was on her feet the day after surgery. That morning her older son came in to see her and was delighted at how well she looked.

A medical student, he was the first to be told his mother had a malignancy. He went home to tell his father. According to Deane, the whole experience was a good one for him, for it gave him a greater compassion for people's mental and spiritual needs as well as their physical needs. "He's going to be a good doctor!" Deane told me.

"Financially those months of trial were not good for us," she said, "but spiritually they were the best we ever had. Through them we learned to love and trust the Lord more and more."

Most of us Christians may glibly give mental assent to Romans 8:28, but do we really believe that God will work all things for good for them that love Him? When we truly accept the truth of that, as Deane did, then we can sleep easily at night and trust everything to our Lord's omnipotent hand.

HUSBANDS

Bea and Deane were in despair because of

health problems, but there are many other problems that send women down to the depths of despair, too. Husbands, children, and other family members can cause us much grief. A woman's husband may drink and gamble, he may be abusive physically or verbally, he may run around with other women. A number of women I have know have lived under such conditions for years. How do they rise up from under the burden of despair?

One friend of mine had a husband who made life a hades on earth for her and her children because of his drinking and gambling. One night when he came home drunk he even threw a knife at his 12-year-old daughter, narrowly missing her. My friend sought her solace from the Lord. She had time of daily devotions with her children every evening as they gathered around her bed.

Sometimes she too fell down before despair. She would call me on the phone seeking encouragement and counsel. I would share with her reassuring verses from God's Word and pray with her. The Bible says, "Bear ye one another's burdens, and so fulfill the law of Christ" (Gal. 6:2).

Because I myself had been down a long, trying road in life, I could understand something of what she was going through. The Lord gave me just what to say. Often she would exclaim at the end of our conversation, "Oh, Muriel, I feel better now. The turmoil in my heart has been eased." Why was that? Because she believed the precious promises of God that I shared with her from Psalm 34 and other Scriptures. And because she continued to believe, God answered her prayers. Her husband is now a dedicated man of God, and they at last have a home of love and harmony.

Things don't always work out this way, however. If God knows a man is not going to change, He may choose to deliver a woman and her children from a life worse than death, from a situation that is dangerous to their physical, mental, spiritual, and moral well-being.

Dr. G. Campbell Moran, in his book *Life's Problems*, says, "Remember, you never touch a man without influencing him. . . . To exert a destructive influence is the most terrible sin that is possible to any man." He advised such a man to either go to the source of purification, God; or take himself away from home, friends, and society and go to live in a desert place, "in order that the foul influence of your soul may not contaminate other men."

God may deliver a woman and her children from such a man, as the woman cries for His help day after day. He may either take the man away by death, or cause him by circumstances to desert his family in a way that their lives would not be endangered by his temper. I don't believe it is God's will for a woman to expose her children and herself to a life of violence, abuse, degradation, and exposure to continual bad influence. In the law of Moses God allowed divorce because of the hardness of men's hearts, according to Jesus (Matt. 19:8).

Another friend of mine often called me, and she too was relieved by being reminded of God's promises. As she believed them, peace came. Her problem was that her husband gambled away the money they had set aside to pay the bills and buy food with. Of course it was a terrible trial every time this happened. But this woman learned to commit the needs of the family to the Lord; and He met them as she trusted Him and believed that "my God shall supply all your need according to his riches in glory by Christ Jesus" (Phil. 4:19).

HOPE FOR ALL WOMEN

What about women who have not yet come to know Christ as their Savior? Can they too find deliverance from despair? Or course they can, for God loves them, too. If ever there was a loser, it was the woman who met Jesus at the well in Samaria (John 4). She had no doubt known plenty of heartache and despair in her life. She had had five husbands and the man she was living with when she met Jesus hadn't even bothered to marry her.

No Pharisee of the Jews would have lowered himself to talk to that woman. Few ordinary Jews would have done so. She would have been beneath their contempt, being a Samaritan. But Jesus, even though He knew all her past, spoke to her kindly and told her He would give her living water.

"But whosoever drinketh of the water that I shall give him shall never thirst," He told her, "but the water that I shall give him shall be in him a well of water springing up into everlasting life" (John 4:14).

When Jesus revealed that He knew about her marital situations and yet went on to share some great truths with her, she suddenly realized that He must be the Messiah that had been promised. He acknowledged that He was.

At that moment she must have received the living water of eternal life from Jesus. She believed; for quickly she ran back to the city and spread the word that Christ was at the well. The Samaritans came out to listen to Jesus, and many of them believed.

If Christ knew that woman's past, then He knew her future. He was not one to waste words. Most certainly she became Christ's disciple and an heir to eternal life. Most certainly her life must have been wondrously changed from a life of failure and despair with men to a life that bubbled over with the water of life.

I have interviewed many women whose lives have been changed like that in recent years. Christ is still in the life-changing business. He still gives hope in times of despair. He still gives joy to those in sorrow. He still gives the abundant life to all who will truly believe in Him and give their hearts to Him.

Christ did not promise His disciples an easy life in this world. He said to them, "These things I have spoken unto you, that in *me* ye might have peace. In the world ye shall have tribulation; but be of good cheer; I have overcome the world" (John 16:33).

John, Christ's beloved disciple, wrote, "And this is the victory that overcometh the world, even our faith" (1 John 5:4).

SOMETHING YOU CAN DO:

1. Read Psalm 34. Before reading, ask the Lord to give you understanding.

2. If you have a desperate burden, take it to the Lord and leave it with Him. Trust Him for guidance. Trust Him to give you sustaining grace day by day. Trust Him to meet all your needs. Trust Him to work out your problem, to deliver you from a situation or feeling of despair.

3. For study or discussion:

(a) How can a person overcome a feeling of despair? (See Psalm 34:5-9, 17-19, 119:165; Proverbs 1:33; Isaiah 26:3-4, 30:15; John 14:27, 16:33; 2 Corinthians 1:3-4; 1 Thessalonians 4:13, 5:17-18.)

(b) How can a person discover God's will concerning the situation in which she finds herself? (Compare Psalm 31:3, 32:8, 37:3-7, 23; Proverbs 3:5-6; Matthew 7:7; John 14:27, 16:13; Philippians 2:13; 1 Thessalonians 4:3; James 1:5.)

5

DELIVERANCE FROM WORRY

Trust in the Lord with all thine heart; and lean not unto thine own understanding. In all thy ways acknowledge him, and he shall direct thy paths.

Proverbs 3:5-6

When I interviewed Corrie Ten Boom, I asked her, "How are your needs provided for? How have you been able to travel around the world?"

"Well, you know," she said, with a twinkle in her eye, "my Father owns the cattle on a thousand hills. Whenever I have any need, I just ask Him to sell a few cows for me!"

With an attitude like that no Christian would ever have to worry. Do we really believe our Father owns the cattle on a thousand hills—that in fact, everything in the universe belongs to Him? Do we really believe that through our faith in His Son, we are His own precious children: heirs of the kingdom, princesses in our Father's house, the bride of His Son?

Some years ago, when I was still quite young in the Lord, my husband and I went through a time of trial. He was out of work, and the only income we had was from an office job I had just found.

As I drove to work one morning, I was worrying. How were we going to meet the payments on our new house and car? I came to a main intersection and stopped. Quickly glancing up and down the road, I pulled out. Suddenly I heard the screeching of brakes and a sickening crunch. I had collided with a car that had seemed to come out of nowhere.

I received a large repair bill from the driver of the other car a few days later. Since we couldn't pay it, the man sued me.

Of course I prayed about the problem during the entire time, but I didn't yet know about the secret of committing my burdens to the Lord. I worried almost constantly about not only this problem, but all the other financial burdens we had, too.

The Sunday after we were sued our pastor quoted Philippians 4:7 for the benediction: "And the peace of God, which passeth all understanding, shall keep your hearts and minds through Christ Jesus."

Those words really hit me. *I'm sure not experiencing that peace*, I thought. When I got home, I looked in my Bible for the key to having it. Verse six held it! "Be careful of nothing; but in every thing by prayer and supplication with thanksgiving let your requests be made known unto God."

I thought about that verse. I was not to be anxious about anything. I was to bring everything to the Lord in prayer with thanksgiving. I fell to my knees and did just that. Thanking Him for all He had done for us already, I brought all our problems to Him and left them with Him. What a relief I felt then! Faith moved into my heart to banish all my fears and worries. I had God's "peace that passeth all understanding." I knew He was going to help us.

As I arose from my knees, a thought came to me: *Why don't you call the man you hit and explain your situation? He might settle for a lesser sum.*

I called the man. When he heard about our situation, he agreed to cancel the suit and settle for $20. Several days later my husband found another job.

Since that time the secret of having victory over worry through faith in my Lord has carried me through every trouble and emergency. The Lord guides us and answers our prayers when we come to Him in faith, believing and trusting Him.

SHARING THE SECRET

About seven years later, when I was visiting a friend of mine in New Jersey, I was able to share this great truth with her. One afternoon she seemed most distressed. "What's the matter, Marian?" I asked. "Can I be of any help?"

"No, I don't know if anything can help," she

answered. "I'm so concerned about that boy of mine. He just can't seem to make it at school. Sometimes I think I'll go out of my mind worrying about him!"

I put my arm around her and said, "The Lord doesn't want His children to fret so about things, Marian. Have you taken this problem to Him?"

"Oh, of course I have. But I'm still worried sick!"

"When you took the problem to Him, did you trust Him with it?" I asked. "Or when you arose from your knees, did you still carry it on your back?"

Marian's face lit up with understanding. "I see what you mean!" she exclaimed. "Pray with me, will you, right now?"

Together we knelt by her couch. When we arose, Marian's face was serene. "I left it with Him this time, Muriel, and I feel so much better now."

Years later Marian told me that that day was the beginning of a new way of life for her, one of taking her burdens to the Lord and really trusting Him for their disposal. Her son attended a Bible institute when he grew up, where he met the lovely Christian girl he married. He is now a faithful servant of the Lord's.

A PROBLEM CLOSE TO THE HEART

Another woman I know had a problem with a rebellious teenage daughter. Instead of daily bringing this problem to the Lord, Betty became very afraid. "I couldn't trust God with this," she told me. "It was too close to me. I had to handle the problem myself." Betty's way of handling it was to worry constantly about her beloved child and use Scriptures on her like a whip, instead of giving the girl the love and understanding she desperately needed.

One day Cindy tossed her long blond hair back, narrowed her big blue eyes, and cried defiantly, "I'm going to do whatever I want to do!"

Cindy had already begun to run around with the wrong type of friends. During the two years that followed, she ran away from home several times, which made Betty sick with worry. When Betty discovered her daughter was using marijuana, that was the last straw. Betty came to an end of herself.

Getting down on her knees, she said, "God I give up. Yes, God, I give the whole thing over to You!"

"I don't know why we Christians put off so long crying to the Lord and surrendering problems to Him," Betty told me. "The very next day my whole attitude had changed toward my daughter."

That week Betty went to a Bible study class and felt led to speak to the teacher about her daughter. "There are two things people cannot fight, Betty," he said. "One is love and the other is prayer."

As Betty read First Corinthians 13 later that week, she realized how far short she had fallen of showing her daughter the kind of love God shows to us. She asked the Lord to put in her heart so much love toward Cindy that it would break down the wall between them. She sought the Lord's guidance through the many dark days that still lay ahead, and He gave it.

As she released the problem of her daughter into God's hands, she stopped worrying as she had in the past. Crises continued to develop, but Betty believed God, that He was going to work things out. And He did. He also showed Betty a number of ways in which she could demonstrate real love toward her daughter. Today there exists a beautiful relationship between Betty and her daughter, and the fine young man her daughter married.

BELIEVING GOD FOR EVERY NEED

Linda Cawthon of Taylors, South Carolina, was suddenly left a widow with two small children to support. Her husband Jay had been killed instantly in an automobile accident. Still in his twenties, he hadn't thought of making a will. Everything they had was frozen in the estate. Linda would have no income at all until the social security payments started.

Two weeks after Jay's death Linda received an electric bill for $60. She fell to her knees. "Lord, I have a $60 light bill here and I have no money," she exclaimed. "You have allowed my husband to be taken. I am trusting You to pay this."

Two hours later a neighbor Linda hardly knew came by. "Linda," he said, "the Lord laid it on my heart to bring you this money." He pressed a wad of bills into her hand. She opened her hand and looked: three $20 bills!

Sunday after Sunday she barely had enough money for gas to get to church. But when she came home, she would find a $5 or $10 bill someone had stuck into her Bible or pocket.

Several weeks after Jay's death Linda began to run out of groceries. She got on her knees and said matter-of-factly, "Lord, I need cereal, coffee, flour, sugar, soap powder, milk, meat, and vegetables."

The next day two ladies she hardly knew came by her door with bags of groceries in their arms. "We didn't know if you needed these or not," they said, "but we felt the Lord would have us bring them to you."

Everything Linda had asked the Lord for was in those bags, and more.

After each gift from the Lord, Linda would go back on her knees and thank Him. This went on for two months, and then she received her first social security check. After that she had enough to live on, and all the miracles stopped. But God had honored the faith of this young woman who believed and had met all her needs. He even gave her another fine Christian husband two years later.

IN EVERYTHING GIVE THANKS

Another woman who truly believes the Lord for everything is my friend, Vivian Weller. During the past several years Vivian has shared with me about a dozen true experience stories of exciting adventures she has had with the Lord.

Vivian's husband John is also a dedicated Christian. He is a vice president with the Bigelow-Sanford Company. When the Wellers went to Rome with about 600 dealers and their wives, they had an interesting experience. John lost his wallet with all their money and credit cards in the vicinity of "St. Paul's prison."

After searching the area in vain, they were told by the guide to go to the police station and report their loss. Someone gave them $3 and they were dropped off at the station as the tour continued without them. The police, however, were plainly disinterested and wouldn't even try to help the Wellers. John felt frustrated.

"Wait here," Vivian suggested. "Jesus and I are going to find someone to help us." She prayed briefly and left the station.

As she stood outside wondering how the Lord was going to help them, she saw a tall man approaching. She went up to him and told him about their dilemma. He asked her to come with him into the station. Everyone inside immediately jumped to attention as they entered. The man registered their report and then referred them to the American embassy. They caught a bus. The bus driver wouldn't accept the dollar John offered him; he wanted coins. But he closed the door and the bus took off with a lurch.

Vivian felt concern rise in her heart and she saw

concern in John's face. She started singing a gospel chorus: "In everything give thanks, for this is the will of God in Christ Jesus concerning you." John joined her in singing. Soon they were laughing as well as singing, to think what a ridiculous situation they had gotten into. The people on the bus began to laugh with them.

Suddenly the bus stopped. They were at the American embassy. Still not knowing how to pay for the ride, they got off the bus. "Teek-et," the driver called after them. "Tee-ket!" Visions of going to jail came to Vivian, but what could they do? They walked briskly toward the embassy, singing their song again. At the embassy the clerk gave them little hope of getting the wallet back, however.

When they got back to their room about three o'clock Vivian and John prayed together about the matter. Vivian told me, "We felt a little silly, praying about an impossibility. But isn't our Lord able to do the impossible?"

At 3:25 the phone rang. It was the police station. A nun had returned John's wallet. "We knew it was a miracle of God," Vivian said, "for there are 17 police stations in Rome and over a million and a half people. This nun had returned John's wallet to the very station where we had reported the loss."

All the money and credit cards were still in the wallet. One night when the Wellers attended a prayer meeting in Rome, John told about the wallet. Everyone started laughing. "Don't you know," they said, "the biggest miracle of all was that the police returned the wallet?"

Vivian and John could have worried themselves sick over losing all their money and credit cards in a foreign country. Instead, they believed their Lord would take care of the matter, and they sang praises and thanks to Him. I have found it to be true in my own life that the more thankful I am to the Lord for what He has already done for me and even for things He has allowed in my life that I haven't understood, the more wonderful answers to prayers I have seen.

Our Lord Jesus gave the formula for deliverance from anxiety. He said to His disciples, "Therefore take no thought, saying, What shall we eat? or, What shall we drink? or, Wherewithall shall we be clothed? (For after all these things do the Gentiles seek.) For your heavenly Father knoweth that ye have need of all these things. But seek ye first the kingdom of God, and his righteousness; and all these things shall be added unto you" (Matt. 6:31-33).

If you put God first in your life, you will have no need to worry—ever.

SOMETHING YOU CAN DO:

1. Read Philippians 4:4-20. Ask the Lord to help you see the beautiful gems He has for you in this passage of Scripture.

2. Take all your worries to the Lord and trust Him with them. Memorize some of the Scripture given in this chapter and quote them to yourself.

3. For study or discussion:

(a) How can a person stop being anxious about problems? (In addition to Philippians 4:4-20, see Psalms 42:5, 50:14-15, 105:1, 5; Habakkuk 3:17-18; Matthew 6:25-34; Ephesians 1:3, 3:20, 5:19; James 1:2-5; 1 Peter 5:7).

(b) How and why does having faith in God deliver a person from worry?

6

DELIVERANCE FROM FEAR

I sought the Lord and he heard me and delivered me from all my fear.

Psalm 34:4

Fear is a twin of worry. Whereas worry is a nagger, fear is an alarm, a painful emotion of dread. It fills the heart with anxious concern. It can cause panic, and thus lead to dire consequences because of things we do and say when thus possessed. The Lord no more wants His children to be victims of fear than of worry.

There is room for two kinds of fear in the life of a child of God, however. Dr. Paul Brand, well-known Christian hand surgeon and former missionary to India, said, "When used properly, fear, too, is an absolute essential element of human life, a protective instinct without which the human race would never have survived. A mother isn't happy to leave a baby alone until it is grown to have a healthy fear of fire or fear of heights. Fear also supplies, through adrenalin, increased heart rates and other mechanisms to tap abnormal reserves of strength. The trick is to have the right amount of fear, and to control it properly.*

In the Old Testament there are half a dozen Hebrew words translated "fear." The Hebrew word *yare'* is used concerning reverential awe of God or the fear of which Dr. Brand speaks. The Hebrew root word *maguwr* carries the meaning of terror, and this word is used in Psalm 34:4, which is quoted above. In the various contexts in which this word is used in the Old Testament, it seems to mean things we are afraid might happen any minute or in the future. It is that kind of anxious concern the Lord would deliver us from as we trust Him.

Concerning fear, Jesus said to His disciples, "And fear not them which kill the body, but are not able to kill the soul; but rather fear him which is able to destroy both soul and body in hell. Are not two sparrows sold for a farthing? and one of them shall not fall on the ground without your Father. But the very hairs of your head are all numbered. Fear ye not therefore, ye are of more value than many sparrows" (Matt. 10:28-31).

If our times are in His hands (Ps. 31:15), what have we to fear? True, we may be temporarily assailed with doubts and fears; but as David did, we

---

*From an interview given to *Eternity* Magazine, © 1978.

can run to the Lord (Ps. 34:4). He is the great deliverer for those who trust in Him.

FEAR OF THE UNKNOWN

After Linda Cawthon attended her husband's funeral, she went home with her two little children to a big empty house. She had gone through many terrible trials with the help and comfort of her husband, Jay. First, both her grandparents had died. A year later she had seen her father shoot her mother, who had died in her arms.

A tumor had caused her father to go berserk. After it had been shrunk and he realized what he had done, he gave his heart to the Lord. But his trial for murder had been a harrowing experience for Linda, and she had lost her first child. A year later her father died, his body filled with cancer. Linda had lost three more babies before finally giving birth to two healthy children. Now she had suddenly lost her beloved husband through a car accident.

All these experiences had left Linda with a great fear of the unknown, a fear of being alone at night. She knelt there by her bed that night after the funeral and prayed to the Lord. After reading her Bible, she crawled into bed.

She lay there, wide awake. Suddenly she heard a noise at the window. Fear paralyzed her.

Then a still small voice seemed to say, "Linda, get your Bible."

Afraid to turn on the light, she knelt with her

Bible by the nightlight near her bed. It fell open at the Book of Proverbs and one verse stood out: "Trust in the Lord with all thine heart and lean not unto thine own understanding" (Prov. 3:5).

"Don't try to understand why all these things have happened to you," the Lord seemed to say. "Just trust me."

Linda flipped a page and God gave her another verse: "When thou liest down, thou shalt not be afraid: yea, thou shalt lie down, and thy sleep shall be sweet" (Prov. 3:24). *How wonderful!* Linda thought. *I didn't know there was a verse like that in the Bible!*

Believing God's promises, Linda claimed them. She crawled into bed, and for the first time in years she fell instantly asleep. She has never been troubled with fear at night since then.

FEAR IN OUR CHILDREN

I know what it is to deal with fear myself—not for myself, but for my younger daughter. From an early age Lori has been an extremely talented and creative person. When she was four she won first prize in an art contest for children. Her wonderful imagination has never failed to amaze me.

This same imagination led her—and me—through a nightmare existence. For three years getting Lori to bed was a struggle. Abnormally afraid of the dark, she imagined all kinds of monsters in her room, although I left the door open.

She was also especially afraid of the bathroom

for some reason. After we heard a missionary from South America speak, she imagined that vicious piranha fish were in the toilet bowl or the bathtub. You can imagine the problem that caused!

I tried to sympathize with Lori, for I realized what a sensitive child she was. I prayed desperately for wisdom to handle the problems her fears caused. Often at bedtime I would read or quote such Scriptures to her as Psalms 27:1 and 34:4.

Lori's fears even affected her social life. When she attended a Halloween party, ghost stories told by her friend's mother terrified her. She came home in a state of near hysteria. That night I had all I could do to get her to bed. "I'm scared, Mommy," she cried pitifully. "I'm scared!"

When I told the other mother about Lori's fear the next day, she just laughed it off. "My children are never frightened by such stories," she said. "What's wrong with Lori?"

"I don't know," I answered.

Reluctantly, I called our community's mental health clinic, explaining Lori's problem with fear and requesting an appointment. The earliest opening was four weeks away. In the days that followed, however, I felt uneasy about this step.

"Is this not Your will, Lord?" I asked. Then I received a strong impression which I felt was from Him. "The opposite of fear is faith." Faith was the answer.

Lori had recently been asking me, "Mommy, is there really a God?" Lori had made a decision for

Christ, but I began to wonder if it had been genuine. I started praying that if it hadn't, she would come through to a genuine faith in Christ; or if it had, that her faith would be strengthened.

I called the clinic and cancelled Lori's appointment. I believed with all my heart the Lord was going to handle her problem in His way.

One Sunday evening about a month later Lori and I started home from a "gospel sing" service at our church. Several Christians there had testified to the victories that Christ had won in their lives. Pastor Sanders had completed the service with a short, hard-hitting salvation message.

As I pulled the car out of the parking lot, Lori exclaimed tearfully, "Mommy, I'm not sure I'm really saved. I feel lost!"

"Then, honey, the only thing to do is to ask the Lord to forgive your sins," I said. "I know you have done that before, but maybe it was just with your mouth and not with your heart. Do you want to receive the Lord Jesus as your Savior now?"

"Yes, Mommy, I do," she replied.

I pulled to the side of the road and we prayed together.

"Mommy," Lori almost shouted, "I'm so happy! I can't keep from crying, I'm so happy!"

As we drove home Lori looked out at the once-foreboding nighttime scene, dark trees outlined against a blue-black sky, and exclaimed, "Everything is so beautiful. I never saw it so beautiful!"

I knew the miracle I had prayed for had happened. That night Lori's obsessive fears disappeared. She was so thrilled with the Lord that we talked about His Word for an hour before she went to sleep. She had to express her thanks to God for His wonderful salvation, and she prayed spontaneously for the first time that night. She went to sleep with absolutely no trace of fear; and the fear of piranha fish also disappeared.

I know that what the Lord did for my Lori He can do for others!

My friend Jean Westfall had a similar problem with her son John, who was also a sensitive child. When he was eight he became full of fear when he went to bed at night. Jean would soothe him and finally he would go to sleep.

One night John awoke crying. Jean ran into his bedroom. "I had a nightmare!" John bawled. "I'm afraid!"

When Jean asked him to tell her what he was afraid of, he wouldn't. So she shared with him that when she was a little girl she had been afraid a bear would come into her room. John opened up then and shared his fears with her and she comforted him.

We can't go on like this, Jean thought. The next day while she was reading her Bible in Isaiah, it suddenly occurred to her how many verses contained the words, "Fear not."

"Lord, give me Scripture for John now," she

prayed. She continued to read in Isaiah. A verse stood out.

"Fear thou not; for I am with thee; be not dismayed; for I am thy God: I will strengthen thee; yea, I will help thee; yea, I will uphold thee with the right hand of my righteousness" (41:10). Jean underlined that and several other verses in John's Bible and showed them to him that night.

"Remember, John," she said, "God wrote these promises for you, and you can believe what they say. Jesus knew His little children might be afraid and wrote all through the Bible, 'Fear not.' "

Jean had John read the verses after her. They did that every night for two weeks. "As God's Word took hold of John's mind, his fears completely subsided," Jean told me. "Never again has John been afraid of the night. He knows that Christ is with him."

PHOBIAS

Other fears may assail us as we grow older. My psychology teacher at a Christian university said that everyone has at least one phobia, which is an irrational, persistent fear of a certain thing such as height, being enclosed, dogs, cats, or darkness.

I used to feel somewhat that way about spiders and still do when a huge one runs right toward me. When my husband pastored a church in the ridge country of southwestern Wisconsin, our parsonage was a tin-roofed stucco shack which we heated with a wood stove in the living room: We had what I called "hot-and-cold running" spiders, and they were huge black ones. I'd go into the bathroom at night and find one in the bathtub or staring me in the face on the woodwork. I'd go into my daughter Gay's room and find a huge black one on her bed. I would pray and run for the flyswatter. Yes, I sought the Lord about this fear—I had to live with it—and He delivered me.

FACING SURGERY

When we lived in Mesquite, Texas, and I had to have major surgery, the Lord gave me perfect peace concerning the whole thing because I just committed myself to Him. I believed that whatever He did or permitted would work out best for me, for I had had long experience by that time in trusting Him.

Lib Bellwood—one of my neighbors here in Greenville, South Carolina—had had long experience in looking to the Lord also. But when she had major surgery everything seemed to go wrong. She developed a staph infection; her stomach became huge and swollen; the incision was hard and blue. "If that hardness around your incision doesn't go away," her doctor told her, "I will have to operate again." Every day he had to open the incision to drain out a bowlful of pus.

After the operation no one had been allowed to

visit Lib, not even her husband. She became depressed and fearful. *"Am I going to die?"* she wondered. On the fourth day after the operation she called her husband. "Honey, I miss you so much!" she cried. "I'm so upset and lonely right now!"

"I know, I know, Lib," he consoled. "I miss you, too. But let's just keep looking to the Lord. Everything will be all right. Just have faith."

After they talked for a while, Lib set the phone back in its cradle. She looked out the window and thought about what her husband had said. She thought about the Lord. "Oh, Father!" she sobbed softly, throwing herself upon Him.

Suddenly something happened. It seemed to Lib as if the Lord just took her into His loving arms right then and said, "You are not alone. I am with you."

A wonderful peace filled her whole being, banishing fear and depression. She knew the Lord was with her and she wasn't going to die. Although her stomach had to be drained every day and she lay in isolation for a total of 14 days, Lib had perfect peace for the rest of her stay in the hospital. She knew her Lord was in there with her all the time and it was precious to her. The staph infection finally cleared up and she was able to go home.

Faith is the answer to fear. Do we really believe God's promises? God's Word will help us to have the faith we need to gain deliverance from fear.

SOMETHING YOU CAN DO:

1. Read Psalm 91. Ask the Lord to help you to truly believe His promises.

2. If you or your child is fearful, use God's Word to increase faith to the point where fear is overcome. Memorize some of the verses quoted in this chapter or listed below.

3. For study or discussion:

(a) What promises in God's Word can help us overcome fear? (See Psalms 23, 27:1, 46:1-2, 145:18; Isaiah 26:3, 41:10-14, 43:1-7; John 14:1-3, 27.)

(b) Think through the fears you have. Why do you have them? What experiences in the past may have put these fears into your mind? Is there any reason you should have them now, when you know God's hand is on every detail of your life? Ask the Lord to help you to understand the basis of your fears and then to dismiss them.

7

DELIVERANCE FROM HEALTH PROBLEMS

And the prayer of faith shall save the sick, and the Lord shall raise him up.

James 5:15

Some sincere Christians believe that as long as you have faith you can be delivered from any physical affliction or illness. But I have had enough evidence close at hand to know that this is not always true. However, if it is not God's will to deliver one of His children from a vale of suffering, He goes with that child through it and uses that beloved one for His glory, if that child will just look to Him.

My own dear father had tremendous faith in the Lord. He believed with all his heart that God could heal him. During his first bout with lung cancer in 1977 Dad received cobalt treatments to shrink the tumor. One Sunday afternoon he and Mother went to the Greenville Memorial Auditorium where an evangelist said to have the gift of healing was preaching. Dad went up to be prayed over. He came home fully believing he was healed.

I had had the people of my church praying for Dad, too; and a number of them are real prayer warriors. But, a year after his first stay in the hospital, my father died at the age of 79, his body filled with cancer and vascular disease.

That experience has not weakened my faith one bit that God heals in answer to believing prayer. I knew even before that that the Lord had not chosen to heal my dearest friend, Bea Fishter, whose body was slowly destroyed by rheumatic arthritis and the cortisone given her to relieve it. She also died and went to be with the Lord.

The Bible says, "Devout men are taken away and no one understands that the righteous are taken away to be spared from evil. Those who walk uprightly enter into peace" (Isa. 57:1-2). It is a blessing to go to be with the Lord (Phil. 1:21-23).

Does this mean we should not pray for physical healing and believe God for it? Of course not. The Lord has healed many people in answer to prayer, as they believed. Jesus Christ is the same yesterday, today, and forever (Heb. 13:8). He healed people when He walked the earth; He heals today. His Spirit lives in His people today, and they too can be healed and delivered from death *if it is His will*.

There are times when the Lord is glorified more in lives by infirmities, distresses, and even death than by deliverance from these things (John 9:1-3; 2 Corinthians 12:9-10). When the five missionaries were killed by the Auca Indians in Ecuador some years ago, thousands of young people dedicated their lives to go to the mission field because of their deaths; and the whole tribe of Aucas were reached for Christ.

"For my thoughts are not your thoughts," God says in Isaiah 55:8, "neither are your ways my ways." Some things are more important in God's sight than our physical healing: our becoming "dead to self"; our being "crucified with Christ" and conformed to His image; our lives being used to His glory and the salvation of others; our eternal welfare.

The Lord also knows the future and we do not. If He chooses not to heal us, He will give us grace and peace that passeth all understanding if we just trust in Him. Jesus said, "In the world you shall have tribulation; but be of good cheer; I have overcome the world" (John 16:33). This world is only a brief moment of the eternity we will spend with our Lord Jesus Christ!

BELIEVING GOD FOR WISDOM AND HEALING

Having said all that, let me share the other side. I myself have believed God for healing a number of times in my own life, and He has worked in a number of ways.

For about a year and a half I was troubled by a bronchial problem. Whenever I sang or spoke in public I felt like coughing. Whenever I was interviewed on television or radio, I had to lean hard on the Lord; and He enabled me to get through the interview without coughing.

I went to the doctor several times, because I had had chronic bronchial problems off and on for some years. None of his prescriptions helped me. Since I sneezed a lot also I began to suspect it was some kind of allergy. The nearest recommended allergist was in North Carolina, and several people I knew who had allergies and went there had to take the long trip periodically and still hadn't gotten complete relief.

Of course I prayed a lot about my problem. I also had a group of dedicated Christians pray over me. I asked the Lord to show me what I was allergic to, and He did. I was allergic to two things: certain kinds of ink used in printing (that figures!) and the grass clippings I had put on my garden to mulch it. I asked the Lord to direct me as to anything I could do or take to alleviate the problem. Of course awareness of what I reacted to helped me a lot. But then I read in *Prevention* magazine that 50 mg. of pantothenic acid a day was found to have helped people with allergies. I began taking a tablet every day, along with 250 mg. of Vitamin C and Brewers yeast.

I don't know if that was what did it, or if the Lord finally chose to answer my prayers, but my problem cleared up. I gave God all the glory.

Sometimes as we believe God for an answer, He

does lead us to do something. Do you recall how Jesus anointed the eyes of a blind man with clay and then sent him to wash it off in the pool of Siloam? (John 9:1-8).

A verse I claimed during the time of my bronchial trouble was Mark 11:24: "Therefore I say unto you, What things soever ye desire, when ye pray, believe that ye receive them, and ye shall have them." That's a great promise! I memorized it and still quote it to myself from time to time.

JESUS STILL DOES MIRACLES

Tamra Wilson—who during her senior year at Hillcrest High in Simpsonville, South Carolina, had been voted "Homecoming Queen"—heard the sentence of death pronounced on her on her eighteenth birthday. As she lay in a hospital bed the doctor told her she had leukemia, and she knew she was going to die.

Panic struck her. "Am I going to Heaven, or am I going to Hell? Oh, God, do I really know You?" Tamra looked up at the doctor and asked for her pastor.

"He's right outside," the doctor said.

Although Tamra had made a profession of faith in Christ when she was 12, she wasn't at all sure it had been real. It had just been the thing to do in her church. Everybody did it. Now it didn't seem enough.

Tamra thought she had a fatal disease, and she was right. Just the night before the doctor told her what she had, he had told her parents that she would die within six months.

A large group of young people had come that night with a cake and presents to help Tamra celebrate her birthday. Later, as they were leaving, Tamra's mother took them aside and told them the bad news. "Pray with me for Tamra," she said. There in the waiting room of the hospital they all fell to their knees, crying and praying to God for their dying friend. Some got right with the Lord.

The next morning when Tamra's mother awoke she was overcome by the realization that very soon Tamra would hear she had a fatal disease. She raised her hands up to the Lord and cried, "God, help me!"

Something seemed to go right through her then, and she knew beyond a shadow of a doubt that God was going to heal Tamra. She was so happy and thrilled with the revelation that she started crying with joy.

After the doctor told Tamra about her having leukemia, Tamra's mother and her pastor, Bill McDonald, went in to see her. "Tamra," her mother said, gripping her shoulder, "do you know Jesus?"

"Yes, ma'am, I know Jesus."

"Jesus is going to heal you, honey. Do you believe that?"

Tamra told me that was rather hard for her to believe because she didn't know Jesus did things like that today. But she answered, "I want to believe that."

"Well, believe it," her mother said, "because it's true. And there's a Scripture about anointing with oil. This won't get you well. It's a symbol of your faith in the Lord. Would you like to have it done?"

"Yes, ma'am. I'd like to have it done," Tamra agreed.

Pastor McDonald started to anoint Tamra's head with oil and pray over her, but Tamra didn't remember any of it. She told me it just seemed as if the Lord picked her up and held her in His arms just then. "When my pastor finished praying, my fear was gone," she said. "My heart was filled with a peace and joy such as I had never known before. For the first time in my life I knew that Jesus was real, He was alive, and He really had come and died on the cross for my sins. And I knew He loved me!"

Tamra was transferred that day to the Emory University Medical Center in Atlanta, Georgia, which has extensive research facilities and many cancer patients. There a doctor took her parents aside and said, "I would advise you to buy a book on death and dying and acceptance of it, with the kind of leukemia your daughter has."

But within three days Tamra was well enough to get up. She and her mother went all around the fifth floor, praising the Lord and testifying to other patients. Tamra's white blood cell count had gone down from 260,000 to 3,000, even though she hadn't yet received any blood or platelet transfusions or cobalt treatments. Eleven days after Tamra heard she had a fatal disease she was back in classes at Hillcrest High. Now six years later Tamra is in the Lord's service.

After hearing Tamra's story I interviewed her pastor, Bill McDonald. I then asked him to pray for my daughter, Lori, and to anoint her with oil. For about five years Lori had been troubled by some kind of problem that had caused her to sniffle and constantly blow her nose. Her pediatrician had passed it off and had said it wasn't an allergy, but he had done nothing to help her. The children at school teased her unmercifully. I had prayed and asked the Lord to help us, and I knew somehow He would.

Bill McDonald and I laid hands on Lori, and he anointed her with oil and prayed. That was five years ago. She has not been troubled with the problem since. Bill and I believed the Lord for Lori and she was healed. At that time Lori had some faith, but what the Lord did for her then increased her faith. She learned to take every problem to the Lord.

A MIRACLE FOR THE DOCTOR

Frances Rogers, a Baptist, lay in the operating room of a hospital awaiting the removal of a malignant tumor in her left breast. The surgeon was late. Frances gazed up at the skylight above her.

"Lord, if any healing takes place," she said,

"You are going to have to do it anyway. The doctor who is scheduled to do this operation doesn't know You or Your healing power. If You would heal me right now, it would be a wonderful way for him to see that there is a Physician greater than he."

Frances felt perfect peace descend on her. Immediately she knew she was healed. When the doctor showed up a few minutes later she told him the Great Physician had healed her and she wasn't going to have the surgery. He called in several other doctors and explained the situation. "Let's look at her x-rays again," one doctor suggested.

"You needn't look at the pictures," Frances said. "They don't apply anymore." To humor her they took her down for some more x-rays.

Frances told me, "I will never forget the look on those doctors' faces when they saw the results! 'She is right!' one doctor exclaimed. 'The lump is gone!'" Frances was released that day and went home.

That night her surgeon called and asked if he might come by with his wife. Frances said they could. She made a list of Scriptures to give the doctor to read. When he arrived, he asked her to tell what had really happened to her and she told him. Then she talked to the doctor and his wife about Jesus and how He had died for our sins, arisen from the grave, and lives today. "You see the evidence that He lives today," she said, "in what He's done for me!"

Several weeks later the surgeon called Frances

again and told her he had read all the verses she had given him. He asked for another list with verses on how to be saved. When he came for the list Frances talked to him again about the Lord and encouraged him to start going to church and to give his life to Christ.

The surgeon's wife called Frances two weeks after that. "We have decided to accept Christ as our Savior," she said. "We're going to start attending church, too." According to Frances, after that this surgeon prayed over every patient on whom he operated.

The Great Physician healed Frances almost 30 years ago and she has never had a recurrence of the tumor.

PSYCHOSOMATIC AILMENTS

Many psychologists and doctors believe that perhaps 75% of people's physical ailments are psychosomatic: that is, they are caused by a person's thinking. They are brought on by the tension caused by worry, fear, hostility, and all kinds of wrong thinking, some of which may stem from childhood experiences.

When I was teaching at the Christian Writers' Conference in Black Mountain, North Carolina, I met Sue Eubanks, a doctor's wife. Sue had been troubled by migraine for years. Her husband had to admit there was very little the medical world could do for her. "I guess you'll just have to learn to live with it, honey," he said.

Sue had been living with the fierce headaches, stomachaches, nausea, and vomiting ever since she had been a young girl. Now she was a married woman with two children. Every time she encountered a stressful situation, it seemed a little voice would say, "You are going to get a headache; you are going to get sick." Knowing what was coming increased her tension.

Although Sue had made a profession of faith in Christ when she was young, it hadn't been a genuine commitment to Him. Deep inside there was a longing to really know the Lord. She prayed to God to help her.

In an art class Sue met a young woman named Rosie, who radiated faith, peace, and joy. One day Rosie related to Sue how the Lord had healed her back after an accident. When Sue told about her migraine, Rosie assured her that God cared for her and could heal her, too. The following night she took Sue to a home prayer meeting to be prayed for.

Sue went to the meeting fully expecting to be healed. The Christians laid hands on her and prayed. In her heart Sue knew God had done something for her.

"Right after they prayed for me," Sue told me, "I turned my life over to the Lord. For when I heard at that meeting that Jesus loved me, that He had died for my sins, and that He would come to live in me if I truly received Him, the Holy Spirit convinced me it was the truth and I believed.

"The Lord started working to deliver me from that very hour," Sue said, "but it was a gradual process. I had to be released from patterns of reaction to stress by learning to trust in the Lord day by day, hour by hour. For the opposite of fear—and that's what really caused my headaches—is faith. God taught me a new way of life, living by faith. I began to meet stressful situations with faith. The migraine attacks started clearing up."

Sue's problem had stemmed from the stressful childhood she had had. But with the Lord's help she had the victory on most occasions after that. "When I took my eyes off the Lord and fell back into my old thought patterns," she told me, "I'd get a migraine attack." Sue has learned to keep her eyes steadfastly on the Lord so that migraine attacks seldom trouble her anymore.

A side benefit of all this has been that family relationships were healed, Sue and her husband have become one in the Spirit, and their marriage became more beautiful than ever. That is what happens in many cases when women truly believe God.

SOMETHING YOU CAN DO:

1. Read James 5:13-18. Was this Scripture written only for the first-century Christians? Or is it for us today also?

2. If you or some loved one has a health problem, ask the Lord for wisdom and insight concerning it. Ask the Lord for healing and believe that He answers such prayers, even as He answers other

prayers (1 John 5:14-15). Or you might feel led to follow the advice God gives in James 5.

3. For study or discussion:

(a) Do you know of anyone who was healed in answer to prayer? Why do good Christians vigorously defend all the miracles described in the Bible, and yet not believe that God will do such miracles today? (See Genesis 11:9, 18:10-14; Exodus 14:21-22; 1 Kings 17:1, 16, 18:37-39; Daniel 3:16-28; Jonah 1:17; Luke 1:13, 18, 26-37; John 11:47, 14:12-14; Acts 6:8; 1 Corinthians 12:9; Hebrews 13:8; Revelation 11:3-6.)

(b) Why does God heal some people and not others? (See Luke 4:27; John 9:1-7; 1 Corinthians 11:29-32; 2 Corinthians 12:7-10; Philippians 2:25-27, 4:14; Hebrews 12:5-11; 1 Peter 1:6-7, 4:12-13; 1 John 5:16.)

8

DELIVERANCE FROM MENTAL AND EMOTIONAL PROBLEMS

For God hath not given us the spirit of fear; but of power, and of love, and of a sound mind.

2 Tim. 1:7

Just as God is able to deliver us from health problems, so He is able to deliver us from mental and emotional problems. And just as many physical problems are brought on by our wrong thinking, even so are many mental and emotional problems.

When we get right with God and really trust in Him, He changes our thinking. We love instead of hate. We forgive instead of holding grudges. We trust instead of doubt. We rejoice instead of grumble. We think of all we can be thankful for rather than all we can complain about.

This new attitude in itself can deliver us from various emotional and mental problems. Faith in God changes us from negative to positive, which has a definite effect on our physical, spiritual, mental, and emotional life. Negative emotions are very much evident in those who are treated by psychiatrists and mental clinics.

MANIC DEPRESSIVE

My friend, Gayle Threlkeld, was full of negative emotions when she allowed herself to be committed to the Marshall I. Pickens Mental Health Center in Greenville, South Carolina. During her last big battle with her husband she had completely lost control of herself and had attacked him. When her doctor called her shortly thereafter and suggested she see a psychiatrist, she was filled with frustration and anger.

I have almost enough pills accumulated now that I can commit suicide, she thought after hanging up the phone. *I even have my farewell note written. What do I want help for? I'm sick of my life. All I want to do is die!*

Sometime later her doctor called back and said, "I spoke to the psychiatrist, and he thinks you should come out to Marshall Pickens for a few days of evaluation." That upset Gayle even more, but finally she yielded to her doctor's persuasions and agreed to go.

As she walked into Marshal Pickens with her husband, negative feelings overwhelmed her. *What am I doing in a place like this?* she wondered. *It's all my husband's fault, and those doctors!* She turned on her husband and glared at him. Through grated teeth she exclaimed, "I hate you!" When her doctor came in she said the same thing to him.

Gayle was diagnosed as manic depressive, according to her physical as well as her emotional symptoms; and she was kept at the hospital for a month. When she was discharged she was taking 24 pills a day and felt like a walking zombie. Every morning nausea overwhelmed her and she couldn't eat breakfast. Having no ambition to do anything, she would go back to bed. Her senses of smell and taste were gone (typical of manic depression). At the end of a week she stopped taking the pills. She came a little out of the fog, but still felt depressed.

Several days later Gayle listlessly sat on the couch in her living room. *What is life all about?* she wondered. *Is this living?*

Suddenly she looked up. "God, please help me!" she cried. Tears began flowing down her cheeks. "Touch me—help me find myself. I can't do it alone anymore. I have tried everything else, God, and it didn't help. Now I'm asking You to help me!"

Gayle got her Bible. It fell open to the Book of Psalms, to verses that told her God would be with her and would help her. How comforting those promises were. Gayle believed them.

Gayle arose and started doing things around the house for the first time in days. The next morning when she got up, she discovered to her joy that the nausea was gone and she could actually eat breakfast with her family. Her senses of taste and smell had returned and the food tasted delicious. Gayle felt good inside.

Several days later Gayle was thinking about the progress she had made. "God," she said in awe, "if You can do this for me, a lowly sinner, someone who is so little and undeserving, then the least I can do is offer my life to You. Come into my heart and life, Lord Jesus!"

"What a difference the Lord has made in my life, Muriel!" Gayle said to me. "The hate and bitterness were replaced with the desire to serve my Lord. I have an entirely new outlook on life. I no longer yell at my children or scream and curse at my husband. The Lord completely cleaned up the foul mouth I used to have!"

Gayle is now a leader in our church. She serves as president of the Women's Missionary Union, teaches Sunday school, and sings with the choir. Every Tuesday she goes to a local rest home and prays, reads the Bible, comforts, and sings for the shut-ins there.

Trusting the Lord delivered Gayle from manic depression and gave her a brand new life.

CANDY'S SEARCH FOR PEACE

Candy Mayer, a Jewish girl, was another who had emotional problems. When she was small her parents took her to a child psychologist. Later, when she was in her teens, they took her to a hypnotherapist. After that, her father, who was a doctor, put her on medication to help her nerves.

She also started having regular sessions with a psychiatrist. But nothing really helped much.

It wasn't until she was 16 that Candy got a glimpse of hope for herself. Her parents' housekeeper, Eleanor Stoppe, was a Christian. One night she took Candy to a Christian youth rally. A line from a song made a special impression on Candy: "Lord, make me whole."

Is being "whole" what makes the difference between Eleanor and me and our families? she wondered.

Not long after that, Candy went to spend the night with the housekeeper and her family. On the way to Eleanor's house two cars careened toward them and narrowly missed them. Eleanor and Candy began talking about death. "If I had died just then," Eleanor told Candy, "I would have gone to Heaven to be with the Lord. I've received Jesus Christ as my Savior."

Although Candy didn't quite understand what Eleanor was talking about, she was intrigued by what she said. They began discussing God and the Bible. In fact, Candy and Eleanor and her husband continued their conversation until late that night. "I want to believe," Candy cried, "but I'm a Jew!"

Around two in the morning Candy felt compelled to look up. "At that moment I saw the Lord!" she told me. "He was reaching His hand out to me. And, oh, His look of compassion and love!"

"Take my hand," the Lord Jesus said to Candy.

"Believe in Me. I'll replace your miserable life and give you peace." Then the vision vanished.

"Eleanor, I believe!" Candy cried.

"What did you say?" she asked.

"I believe!"

"Well, praise the Lord!"

The heavy burden was lifted from Candy's heart. "For the first time in my life I was happy," she told me.

On her last visit to the psychiatrist Candy told him how she had trusted in Christ as her Savior and how He had changed her whole outlook on life. After Candy graduated from high school that spring, she attended a Christian university in Greenville, where I became acquainted with her. I could tell from Candy's radiant countenance that she finally knew what "shalom" meant.

CHILD BEATER

Kay Cherry had a different kind of problem, one that too many men and women in this country have today. She took her anger, frustration, and hostility out on her three active young children.

One day when she was raging with anger, she struck fiercely at her small daughter, who cringed from her blows. Suddenly Kay stopped and looked at her tightly-curled fist in horror. She buried her face in her hands and wept in anguish. *I'm turning into a child beater!* she thought.

Kay had realized for a long time that she had serious emotional problems. She had pored over books and magazines on psychology, trying to find answers.

"I hated myself," she told me. "I had always hated myself. I had had an insecure childhood. As a result, I was plagued by an inferiority complex, depression, loneliness, guilt, uncertainty, a sense of failure, and a distrust of other people. I had lived with these things for years. No wonder I quickly ran out of patience when it came to coping with my three active young children!"

Kay and her husband Art had recently moved from Indiana to South Carolina, and her children seemed to go from one illness to another. She felt lonely in the strange environment far from friends and family. Concerned about his new job and money matters, Art was tense and tired when he came home at night. He and Kay frequently quarreled.

"My nerves seemed stretched to the breaking point," Kay told me. "Then one day, when all the children were crying and I felt I couldn't take anymore, I looked through the window up at the sky and screamed, 'Lord, what's wrong with me?' "

Immediately past incidents flashed into Kay's mind. They all seemed to fit together like a jigsaw puzzle. Someone seemed to say, "Here is what is wrong. Now forget these things. Forgive yourself and live your life."

Kay sat down and cried for a long time. Some of the bitterness seemed to wash away with her tears.

Shortly after that Kay took her children to Sunday school and joined the young women's class. "Those women had something," she told me, "a joy and enthusiasm and love that I almost envied." The following Sunday Kay stayed for the church service and it seemed as if she were hearing the gospel of Christ for the first time. She began to realize that the fact she was a lost sinner was her biggest problem.

Kay started attending a Bible class on Tuesdays. There she heard that Jesus loved her; He had died for her sins. "How can I hate myself if He loved me so much He died for my sins?" she asked herself. As she saw the joy and peace the other women in the class had, she yearned for it herself.

One Tuesday afternoon Kay stood at the kitchen sink thinking about these things. She closed her eyes and prayed, "Jesus, I'm weak. I know I can't live my life myself. Please come into my life, and I'll live for You. I'll even tell others about You, but You'll have to help me, Lord."

"No bolt from the blue struck me," Kay told me. "I felt no great sensation. I simply accepted by faith what the Bible says in Romans 10:13, 'Whosoever shall call upon the name of the Lord shall be saved.'"

That evening when Kay's husband came home he received a pleasant surprise. He was not greeted by the usual discordant din of Kay's angry shouting and the children's cries. Instead, he found Kay singing happily as she finished preparing dinner. The children were playing contentedly. Kay greeted him with a kiss.

"What happened to you?" Art asked in amazement.

"I'm happy," Kay answered. Later that evening she told Art how she had asked Christ to come into her life and He had changed her heart and given her joy. During the days that followed Art could see the amazing change was real. When he commented on Kay's greater love for him and the children, or on her new patience, she would say, "It's Jesus that makes the difference."

About three months later God answered Kay's prayers for her husband, and Art also asked Christ to come into his life.

When I held a four-day Bible club for children at Kay's house about a year after her conversion, she told me, "The hands that I once used to beat my children now reach out to them in love." Not only did they reach out in love to her own children, but to about fifty more in the neighborhood, many of whom came to know Christ as their personal Savior through the four-day and weekly Bible clubs that were held in Kay's home.

FORGIVE YOURSELF

Forgiving one's self as well as others seems to be an important step toward mental and emotional health for many people. As they realize how God forgave them all their sins for Christ's sake (and He will forgive the things we do wrong after we trust in Christ, too), they find it easier to forgive themselves. This was a point I sought to impress on a young woman who looked to me for counsel one summer at the Christian Writers' Conference where I taught.

I pointed Jackie to First John 1:9, which says, "If we confess our sins, he is faithful and just to forgive us our sins, and to cleanse us from all unrighteousness."

"I'm familiar with that verse," she said, "but I can't help hating myself for having made such a mess of my life."

"Jackie, if God forgives us, shouldn't we be willing to forgive ourselves?" I asked her gently. "One of the two great commandments Jesus gave us is, 'Love thy neighbor as thyself.' Do you think you can fully obey that command to love your neighbor as yourself if you don't love yourself? If you hate yourself, it will affect all your relationships with your fellow man, won't it?"

As I continued to talk with Jackie, she began to realize that she had to stop brooding about the past, forgive herself, and go on with the Lord. "Take as your Scripture what the Apostle Paul said in Philippians 3:13, 14," I told her. " 'Forgetting those things which are behind, and reaching forth unto those things which are before, I press toward the mark for the prize of the high calling of God in Christ Jesus.' "

Jackie wrote that and other verses down, and there was a look of hope in her face and a smile on her lips as we parted.

FORGET THE PAST

In some cases we can rectify mistakes we made

in the past, but in others there is little we can do about them except put them under the blood of Christ and go on from there. The Lord can give us a glorious new life if we will only trust Him and walk with Him day by day, seeking His guidance.

When we are filled with God's Spirit, as we yield completely to Him, then we have the fruit of the Spirit: love, joy, peace, patience, goodness, gentleness, meekness, faithfulness, and self-control. A woman filled with these qualities cannot help but be well-balanced mentally and emotionally.

SOMETHING YOU CAN DO:

1. Read Romans 8:1-18. Ask the Lord how applying this passage might help you mentally, emotionally, and spiritually.

2. Does any particular mental or emotional problem bother you? Do you often feel depressed? Is your heart full of hostile feelings toward others? Do you fly off the handle easily and often? Are you troubled with bad thoughts? Call on the Lord and trust Him to help you, as He did the women mentioned in this chapter. What He has done for others, He can do for you.

3. For study or discussion:

(a) Might some emotional or mental problem be caused by a physical problem? How can this be determined? (Cp. 2 Corinthians 12:7-8; Colossians 4:14; 2 Timothy 4:11; James 1:5.)

(b) How can God and His Word help us overcome mental or emotional problems? (See Genesis 18:14; Deuteronomy 6:4-9; Psalm

33:20-22, 78:23-28, 94:17-22; Proverbs 23:7; Jeremiah 33:3; Matthew 22:37-40; 2 Corinthians 4:8-9; Ephesians 3:20; Philippians 4:4-8.)

9

HOPE FOR MARRIAGES

Then the Lord God said, It is not good that the man should be alone. I will make an helper meet for him.

Genesis 2:18

According to recent statistics, 35 percent of all marriages today fail. The United States has the highest divorce rate in the world. And who knows how many couples are struggling on in wretched, quarrel-pocked marriages that often provide horrible examples and homes for their children? God didn't have this in mind when He instituted marriage, but sin has marred the relationships between many husbands and wives.

I have interviewed women who have lived under terrible conditions with their husbands. After being beaten, they have contemplated either killing themselves or their husbands. One woman even set fire to the bed as her husband lay in a drunken stupor. Another woman gulped down a handful of pills and was taken to a mental institution after being released from the hospital.

Would you believe that both of these women and their husbands are in the Lord's service today? Faith in Christ brings hope for marriages.

MARRIAGE WITHOUT CHRIST

My brother Gene and his wife Betty started marriage without Christ. Gene had been reared in Protestant churches, and Betty was a devout Catholic. But neither one of them knew Christ as their personal Savior when they got married.

They were quite happy at first, but after a while a wall developed between them. They seemed to have nothing in common. "Betty was always very tired," Gene told me. "She stopped being a wife to me. As a result I did many things I still regret. Our marriage started falling apart. Our lives became a mess, and we were both miserable!"

I had turned my life over to the Lord shortly before Gene and Betty were married, and during the four years that followed I often talked to them about Christ. One night I said, "If you ever have a real need, go to the Brookdale Baptist Church in Bloomfield." That was not far from their home. My brother went there several times by himself.

My brother was the leader of a dance band, "Gene Koller's Melody Masters," that played for college and church dances in the Newark, New Jersey area. One Saturday night when Gene was out on a dance job, Betty sat home alone worrying about what to do about their marriage. She began talking to God about it. All at once she got the distinct impression that they should start going to church together, that she should offer to go to my brother's church with him. When he came home, she did.

"Well, sure," Gene said, "if you're willing to go to my church with me, I ought to be willing to go!" Since Gene had been to Brookdale several times, that was "his church." They began attending that church almost every Sunday.

Then on Palm Sunday some months later, the church had a guest speaker: Don Robertson of Word of Life. I had often told Gene and Betty about how we need to repent of our sins and receive Jesus Christ as our personal Savior. As they listened to Don Robertson preach and heard this message again, the Holy Spirit opened their eyes fully to their need.

"Romans 5:8 says," the preacher proclaimed, " 'But God commendeth his love toward us, in that, while we were yet sinners, Christ died for us.' "

Both Gene and Betty were convicted that they were lost sinners. That day they realized that Christ was the answer for their crumbling marriage. They went forward in the church that night when an invitation was extended to receive Christ.

The next day Gene and Betty took off for a week in Washington, D.C., for their first real honeymoon. "We got to know each other that week in a way we never had before," my brother told me. "There was a new relationship between us, because Christ was now in our marriage."

My brother enrolled in Northeastern Bible Institute in Essex Fells, New Jersey, that fall. Just before his graduation he was called to pastor a church and was ordained. Later he studied at three other Christian schools, where he earned five degrees, including his doctorate. Presently Gene works as a counsellor with the drug abuse program at Tyndale Air Force Base in Panama City, Florida.

After they had been married for eight years, God gave them their first child and they have had three more. They now have a beautiful relationship. They found from experience that Christ was the answer to their marriage problems. I'm thankful that my sister-in-law sought the Lord, heeded His voice and believed, and obeyed. This response on her part to the living God not only saved her marriage, but resulted in the salvation of her eternal soul, and my brother's.

ABUSIVE HUSBANDS

Recently I read that about one million wives in the United States are beaten or physically abused by their husbands. There probably are no statistics on how many wives are verbally and mentally abused by their husbands—or vice versa. This kind of conduct may spring from mental or emotional illness, alcoholism, inferiority complex, or traumatic childhood experiences.

I cannot truthfully say that all men will be changed by God and believing wives from abusive husbands into kind, gentle men. God does work in lives in answer to prayer. He does transform lives. But He does not force people to live godly lives. He does not force them to stay close to Him, to be filled with His Spirit. Sadly I must admit there are some people who will never come to Jesus Christ and be transformed; and there are other people who do make professions of faith, but who after a time fall back into their old ways of behavior.

Look at the average church and you will see what I mean. Only a comparative few can truly be said to be filled with the Holy Spirit, who gives them power to live in love and harmony with others. Look also at the Israelites, for whom God cared and loved, and yet who turned against Him time after time.

I preface in this way the illustrations I am about to give so that some of you who read this will not have unrealistic hopes and get discouraged. But do have faith in God, for the Bible says, "They cried unto the Lord in their trouble, and he delivered them out of their distresses" (Ps. 107:6). God does deliver His children out of impossible life situations in one way or another.

Carla P. was delivered out of a horrible life situation. Her husband frequently came home drunk and would beat her up, knock her around the room, cursing her. Carla had been a Christian for three years and was praying for her husband's salvation.

One night when he came home late Carla said something to him about their daughter having waited up to see him. He became furious. He followed her into their bedroom, where he began to viciously slap her face back and forth.

Carla cringed in terror at the snarling look on his face. Finally he shoved her into their daughter's room, throwing her across the daughter's bed and waking the child up. By this time Carla's face was swollen, her eyes were black, her ears were ringing and there was a deafening roar in them so that she couldn't hear.

Pinning her down, her husband grated out, "You know I can break every bone in your body, don't you?"

"I know you can," Carla gasped. Their little girl was shaking with fear and crying.

Terrified of her husband, the next day Carla went with her little girl to stay with her mother. Her husband kept calling, trying to get her to come back home. "Lord, he seems so sweet and kind now," Carla prayed, "but I'm still afraid of him. What should I do?"

One morning as she prayed this, the Lord told her, "Go home." When she heard those words, the fear in her heart suddenly disappeared.

Carla went home, and Jim was like a changed person. He gave up drinking and smoking. He started going to all the services of the church with his wife and daughter. He was sweet and kind.

Several months later Carla felt the Lord was dealing with her about being even more of a submissive wife, so she went forward at the altar call.

She felt someone kneeling beside her, taking her hand in his. It was Jim. He was shaking all over. Carla heard him pouring out his heart to God, asking the Lord to save him, receiving Christ as his Savior.

"My husband is so sweet and humble now," Carla told me several years after he was saved. "I can hardly believe he is the man I lived in misery with for so many years. And would you believe the Lord has even given me a real love for my husband? What a sweet relationship a husband and wife can have when Christ is the center of their home!"

UNFAITHFUL HUSBANDS

What does a woman do when she suspects or learns that her husband is unfaithful to her? It's a traumatic experience. Some women rush to the divorce court. But others still love their husbands very much and don't want to give them up without a struggle. Some have tried to forgive their husbands' infidelities, but they find it hard to forget or to trust their husbands in the future. They may live with fear and suspicion.

Christ can and has changed men into faithful husbands, and a number of men have stayed constant for the rest of their lives. But again, I would be unrealistic to say this is always true. In some cases men may get right with the Lord and then backslide to their old ways. A notable example of a man who went berserk over many strange women when he backslid is King Solomon.

But if your husband has changed, or does change through faith in Christ, cover him with prayer and trust the Lord with him. Don't live with fear and suspicion. Give your man the benefit of the doubt.

Elsa B. had good reason to suspect her husband Bill of cheating on her at various times during their marriage. When Elsa learned he was having an affair with his secretary, she faced him with her knowledge. He denied everything. During the months that followed, however, he moved into another bedroom.

After a year and a half of living with the situation, Elsa ended up in the hospital with a condition her family doctor thought must be related to some unendurable life situation.

The hospital psychiatrist came to talk to Elsa. "You've got to face your problems and learn to live with them and forget about it," he told her.

The next day she picked up her "My Daily Bread" booklet. "Take your burdens to the cross and leave them there," was the message for the day. "When Christ arose, He took our burdens with Him."

Well, she thought, *here I am paying a psychiatrist $50 a session just to hear what I've heard in church all my life!* It dawned on her that she could actually turn her problems over to the Lord. He would deal with them and she could forget about them.

"Many times I had taken my burden to the Lord, Muriel," Elsa told me, "but I hadn't really left it with Him. Now I handed it up into His omnipotent hands. Immediately I knew what I had to do."

The burden fell off Elsa's shoulders and she began to recover. When she was discharged from the hospital, she told her husband, "Bill, I love you, but I'm not going to take anymore. You will have to decide between that girl and me!"

A slave to his passion and sin, Bill packed his clothes and left. Elsa stood at the window and watched him leave, tears rolling down her cheeks. But she knew Bill was in God's hands now and she had peace.

Bill lived with the girl for a year and a half, but never asked Elsa for a divorce. Every week he called to talk to her about their sons. Before he would hang up, he always told Elsa he loved her. She just kept praying and trusting the Lord.

After a year and a half of leaning on the Lord and waiting, the call came. "Elsa," Bill said, "do you think you could ever forgive me and take me back?"

"Bill, if you will either get saved or right with

the Lord, I will forgive you and take you back."

"That's the best news I've ever heard!" Bill cried.

Bill went to church with Elsa that Sunday and walked the aisle to rededicate his life to the Lord. According to Elsa, he has been a changed man for the past six years, a faithful husband and devout Christian.

TRANSFORMED WIVES

A number of men have told me that they came to know Christ as their Savior because of their wives, either because their wives had faithfully prayed for them and lived Christ before them, or because the lives of their wives had been transformed by Christ when they had believed in Him.

Jack Matthews, a successful realtor in Fort Lauderdale, Florida, was one man who was astonished and puzzled by the change that had taken place in his wife, Betty. "She seemed to have new values and a new purpose in life," he said. "She had something I didn't have, and so did her new friends. It both puzzled and annoyed me."

During the year that followed Betty's conversion to Christ, she and her friends talked to Jack about the Lord whenever they had the opportunity. Jack didn't like such talk, but Betty was unusually sweet and considerate toward him.

"She mowed our acre of grass and vacuumed

our swimming pool just so that I would have a little more free time," he said. "Not only that, but she kept both our automobiles washed and polished and my shoes neatly shined."

What's going on here? Jack wondered. But he got to the place where he couldn't stand living with such a "religious fanatic." Finally one night he told Betty he would have to ask her for a divorce unless she went back to the way she used to be.

"I love you, Jack," Betty said in a choked voice, "but you don't understand. I have been born into God's family and I can't be unborn. Honey, I'm going to keep praying that God will save you and change your heart as He has mine—and that ours will be a truly Christian home!"

Jack had been very impressed by the dedicated Christian husband of one of Betty's friends. When this man died suddenly, the news of the tragedy shook Jack. At the funeral home the man's wife pulled a tract out of her purse that showed a tombstone and was entitled "Are you ready?"

"Betty, maybe you know someone who is not ready to meet God," she said. "Would you like to give him this tract? It might help him get ready."

"Give me that," Jack exclaimed. "I want to get ready!"

Jack took the pamphlet and several others the widow gave him, and then turned to look at her husband's lifeless body. *If I had been killed instead of him,* he thought, *where would I be now?*

Jack and Betty took their respective cars home.

Two blocks from the funeral home Jack cried out, "God, I want You to save me. I know I'm not ready to die or to meet You. Forgive me for all my stubbornness, all my sin. Come into my heart, please!"

God did. The minute Jack got home he jumped out of his car and ran to Betty's and opened its door. "Honey, will you please come in and pray with me?" he exclaimed. For the first time in their married lives the happy couple went in and knelt by their bed to pray together.

Jack and Betty enrolled in Columbia Bible College to prepare for the mission field. After serving in Africa for a while, they returned to Columbia, South Carolina, where Jack became the dean of men.

I have had the joy of hearing a number of beautiful testimonies like this where men have come to know Christ as their Savior because their wives prayed and believed. Will God save the husbands of some of you who read this if you pray, believe, and follow His leading? Yes, He certainly will!

SOMETHING YOU CAN DO:

1. Read First Corinthians 7:1-16. Ask the Lord what message this passage of Scripture has for you.

2. If you have problems in your marriage, turn them over to the Lord. Seek His wisdom as to what you should do concerning the situations.

3. For study or discussion:

(a) Should a woman stay with her husband no matter how he acts or treats her, or how much her life and those of her children may be endangered? (Cp. Psalm 32:8, 140:1-13; Proverbs 15:16-17, 21:19, 22:24-25, 23:6-7; 1 Corinthians 5:11, 7:10-16, 15:33.)

(b) How can a woman bring about a better relationship between herself and her husband? (See Proverbs 15:1, 25:15, 31:10-12, 26-30; Matthew 7:1-5, 22:39; Romans 12:9-10; 1 Corinthians 7:4-5, 13:1-8, Ephesians 5:22-24; Colossians 3:12-18; 1 Peter 3:1.)

10

WHEN WOMEN WAIT ON GOD

Commit thy way unto the Lord; trust also in him, and he shall bring it to pass.

Psalm 37:5

Sometimes we women thrash about in our own strength and wisdom trying to bring to pass desired goals, and we only succeed in making things worse! We yearn for a husband to be transformed by Christ or a child to get right with the Lord, and we nag and preach and fight. We think we need more money to live on and we rush out to take a job. We want a better house and we get talked into one that will cause us worry every month when the payment is due—and in turn we talk our sceptical husbands into the hazardous deal, too.

The Bible says, "Rest in the Lord and wait patiently for him" (Ps. 37:7).

The Lord can do so much better for us than we can do for ourselves. Jesus said to a friend He esteemed highly, "Martha, Martha, thou art careful and troubled about many things; but one thing is needful, and Mary hath chosen that good part, which shall not be taken away from her" (Luke 10:41-42).

What is that good part? It is looking to Jesus.

The Spirit of Jesus dwells in the hearts of all who have been born again through trusting in Him as Savior. Jesus promised His disciples that after He went back to Heaven, the Holy Spirit would be their teacher and guide. I have learned to look to the Holy Spirit for His guidance in everything I do. I might make mistakes, but He never does!

HOW TO GET A HOME

Back in the early 1970s I had what I felt was a dream that foretold that my father's life would be shortened and my mother would go through a terrible period overshadowed with dark clouds; but she would come out of it comforted by her neighbors. I felt the Lord was leading me to buy a home in my parents' neighborhood, so that I could be close when my parents needed me. I would be one of those neighbors who made things easier.

At that time I was renting a home in another part of Greenville. I told my parents to watch for houses for sale in their neighborhood, and they said they would. I prayed for the Lord to lead me and believed He would.

During the nine months I waited on the Lord, several houses in the neighborhood were put on the market. Each time I looked to the Lord and He said, "Wait."

Then one day Mother called me and said a house up the street was being readied for sale. I drove by to see it. It looked awful on the outside, with brown paint flaking off. But I liked the inside layout—the six large rooms, the fireplace, the back porch, the full attic, the beautiful knotty-pine study with book shelves lining one side. The fenced-in back yard looked like an old-fashioned farmyard, with pecan and apple trees and other decorative trees and bushes.

When I learned the price, I knew I couldn't manage it at all. I had saved some money from the royalties on my books and wanted to buy the equity and take over the 5½% mortgage with the $83-a-month payments. My dad, a retired real estate broker, suggested I make an offer and I did—$4,000 less than the owner was asking. A wealthy and well-known developer in Greenville, the owner acted scandalized. "Well, call me if you change your mind," I said.

"Lady, I'm not going to call you!" he exclaimed, hanging up the phone. I thought to myself, *If the Lord wants me to have that house, he will call me. I know the Lord doesn't want me to burden myself down with a debt that would worry me.* So I prayed and waited.

Both my dad and I had told the owner why I wanted to buy the house, and also about my limited finances. The man, whom I understood was a Christian, called me back a month later. He had come down $2,000 and was willing to loan me $1,000 interest-free for a year so that I could take over the mortgage. "Only you will have to take the house as is," he said, "with it unpainted on the outside and partially painted on the inside."

"I will pray about it and let you know," I said.

I prayed. The thought came to me, *The Lord doesn't want me to worry about money, and if I have to pay $1,000 in a year along with the payments, I might worry.* Furthermore, I felt in my heart the Lord was going to give me that house all painted, inside and out. As much as I wanted it, I continued to wait on the Lord. I knew it wouldn't be put up for sale, until it was all painted.

Several weeks later the owner called again. He had come down to a figure I could manage. But again he said that no more painting would be done on the house. I had seen the men painting on the outside that week. I agreed. The owner said he would check on the house that afternoon and call me back that night.

When he called back, he said, "Well, the men finished the painting on the inside and outside, but I'll let you have it anyway. Come down to my office tomorrow and we'll close the deal."

Since the man was a big contractor, the only extra cost I had was $35 for some closing fee. Oh, I felt like shouting! I was so thrilled to get that house! It turned out to be more perfect for us than I ever could have asked for.

Several years later my dad was found to have cancer. I was there to take Mother to the hospital to see Dad daily and take Dad for cobalt treatments. Later, when he went into the hospital for the two-and-a-half months before he died, I transported Mom back and forth several times a day. My father suffered a lot and it was a terrible time of trial for Mother, just as my dream had foretold. How glad I was to be nearby when my parents needed me! Since Dad went to be with the Lord, I have been Mom's "wheels," because she doesn't drive. Not only was I able to comfort her, but true to my dream, she has often been helped and comforted by our many good neighbors.

Oh, how glad I was that I waited on the Lord!

The story of how God gave me the house appeared in several Sunday school publications, and I sent a copy of it along with some other stories to one of my book publishers, Bible Voice. Carol Candlish, the secretary at Bible Voice, read it. She and her husband, who live in a suburb of Los Angeles, had almost given up hope of buying a home they could afford. When she read what the Lord had done for me, however, Carol believed the Lord could do the same for them, even though it seemed almost an impossibility in that area. Not long after she and her husband turned the matter over completely to the Lord, He led them to exactly the home they had wanted at a price they could afford.

"For with God nothing shall be impossible," the Bible says (Luke 1:37). But you've got to believe it!

TRUST GOD WITH HUSBANDS AND CHILDREN

One area in which we women have a tendency to be most impatient is that which concerns our husbands and children. That's because it's so close to us and can pain our hearts more. We want them to get right with the Lord; we desire better relationships with those who are closest to us. It is hard for us to wait on the Lord in these matters, isn't it?

I know one woman who waited on the Lord for a number of years for her husband to get right with Him. While most of their seven children were growing up, this dear lady endured a terrible time with her husband. He would come home drunk and make life a living hades for his family. He would gamble away the money they needed to pay bills.

The lady loved her husband though and faithfully prayed for him, asking God to work in his life. When the man had an accident that crippled him, he finally got right with the Lord. How wonderfully happy this couple is now! As they look to the Lord together, He supplies all their needs.

Another woman I know was deeply saddened by the wall between her married daughter and herself, a problem I suspect exists between many parents and their children today, a problem often caused because one is following Christ and the other is not.

Jesus Himself predicted this would happen. "Think not that I have come to bring peace on earth," He said. "I came not to bring peace, but a sword. For I have come to set a man at variance against his father, and a daughter against her mother, and the daughter-in-law against her mother-in-law. And a man's foes shall be they of his own household" (Matt. 10:34-36, NIV).

Although Jan had stayed close to the Lord, her daughter had gone far from Him. The more Jan tried to talk to her daughter Sharon about the Lord, the higher the wall grew between them. Jan finally had enough sense to realize she was only antagonizing her daughter; she turned the whole problem over to the Lord. As she prayed, she began to realize there was something else between them, and she asked the Lord to reveal what it was.

God led her to have a heart-to-heart talk with Sharon one day when she was visiting her. Suddenly it all spilled out. Sharon and her husband had had marital problems; they had sought psychiatric help. They finally had seen the "great truth" that their parents were to blame for all their problems!

"You and Dad never really loved me," Sharon accused her mother.

Jan was shocked. She had always loved Sharon dearly, and she knew her husband had, too. But she heard her daughter out, for how can you pray best and act in wisdom toward someone you love unless you know what you're up against?

Jan's heart was leaden as she drove home later

that day, but she knew what she had to do. The reason she had gotten into that discussion with her daughter was because a friend had had a similar problem and had succeeded in breaking down the wall between herself and her daughter with love and understanding. Jan began to pray that the Lord would help her to show special love toward this daughter who had often treated her cruelly in the past.

During the months that followed Jan found many opportunities to show love toward Sharon. She wrote often to her daughter and phoned her regularly long distance. She told her that she loved her. But she soft-pedaled talking about the Lord. She knew her daughter wouldn't listen to her on that until she could win that daughter back to herself.

Finally Jan's big opportunity came. When Sharon had her second baby, Jan offered to help out for a week. Jan threw her whole heart into showing Sharon and her two little ones love. She took care of the older little boy and potty-trained him; and also cared for the baby. She cleaned the house from top to bottom and did whatever Sharon wanted done. At the end of the week when she went home she found on her dining room table a big bouquet from a florist's. With it was a note saying, "With love and gratitude. Thank you, thank you. Lovingly, Sharon."

Love had broken down the wall. Jan and Sharon began to develop a good, loving relationship. Before long Sharon started going to church with her two little ones, praying, and reading her Bible. When Jan took her hands and mouth off the situation, gave it up to the Lord and waited on Him for His direction, the Lord answered and showed her what to do.

YEARNING FOR A CHILD

After I had my first daughter, Gay, I couldn't seem to have another child for a number of years. Oh, how my heart ached whenever I saw a baby in someone else's arms! My unspoken request at every prayer meeting was that God would give me another child. While I was waiting on God, I suffered a miscarriage. But still I knew if it was God's will, He would grant me my request.

Finally, when I was working at Tennessee Valley Authority in Chattanooga, I sent up one last prayer, pleading with the Lord. He answered that prayer and sent me my beloved second daughter, Lori. Looking back, I see that His timing was just right, too.

Sarah had to wait until she was past the age of child-bearing before her prayers for a child were answered. Although she laughed when the Lord finally came and told her husband she would have a son, the Bible lists Sarah with the heroes and heroines of faith in Hebrews 11: "Through faith also Sarah . . . received strength to conceive seed and was delivered of a child when she was past age, because she judged him faithful who had promised" (vs. 11).

Hannah also was barren. She threw herself

completely on the Lord, weeping, promising, and praying (1 Samuel 1:1-17). He answered her request for a son, and that boy became one of the greatest men of God of all time: Samuel. Hannah gave that son to the Lord as she promised; and God gave her three more sons and two daughters.

If the Lord chooses, He can make the barren woman who believes fruitful.

WAITING FOR A HUSBAND, MONEY, OR ANYTHING ELSE

I interviewed a woman who told me that when she and her sister were in their early twenties they wondered if they would ever find Christian husbands. They were tempted to date non-Christians; they didn't want to be old maids. But they decided to rest the matter with the Lord and trust Him concerning it. The Lord led them to take work in a larger city, where they both met their fine future husbands in the larger church they joined there.

Another woman I interviewed had a real financial problem because of the small store she ran. But as she waited on the Lord and prayed, He supplied the exact amount of money she needed, just in time.

I wrote a song which says, "Lean back, and let the Lord take over." There are times in our Christian life when we have to do just that. Just lean back . . . and watch what He will do and how He will lead as we believe in Him.

SOMETHING YOU CAN DO:

1. Read Psalm 62. Ask the Lord to open your eyes to the beauty of its great truths.

2. Ask the Lord for patience to wait for His perfect time for the answer to some prayer. Ask Him for peace of heart if you have some burden.

3. For study or discussion:

(a) How can we tell if something we desire is God's will? (See Psalm 25:5, 9, 32:8, 48:14, 119:105; Isaiah 8:19-20, 30:21; Romans 12:2; Philippians 2:13; James 1:5-6.)

(b) What things can we be sure are in God's will? (See Matthew 6:19-33; John 14:1, 13-15, 23; 15:4, 5, 12; Romans 8:29; 2 Peter 3:9-18.)

11

SALVATION OF LOVED ONES

*Believe on the Lord Jesus Christ, and thou shalt
be saved, and thy house*

Acts 16:31

After we come to know Christ as our personal
Savior, a desire springs into our hearts to see our
loved ones come to know Him, too. As we read
and hear God's Word, we come to realize that
without Christ our loved ones and friends are lost.
Without Christ they will go when they die to the
same place Christ said the rich man went: to a
burning hell (Luke 16:19-31).

When that rich man was there suffering, he
pleaded that someone be sent to his five brothers to
warn them, so that they wouldn't end up where he
was. How much more then does the Holy Spirit lay
the burden for loved ones on the hearts of those
who know and love the Lord?

Let our hearts be cheered by what God's Word
says: "The Lord is not slack concerning his prom-

ise (i.e., that He will come back to earth), . . . but is longsuffering to us-ward, not willing that any should perish, but that all should come to repentance" (2 Peter 3:9). Put that statement of fact together with First John 5:14: "And this is the confidence that we have in him, that, if we ask anything according to his will, he heareth us. And if we know that he hear us, whatsoever we ask, we know that we have the petitions that we desired of him."

PATIENCE AND PERSEVERANCE NEEDED

Some women have had to wait a long time for their prayers to be answered for their loved ones' salvation. Vera Clark waited 24 years, and when the answer to her prayers suddenly came one sunny autumn Saturday, she could hardly believe it.

Vera's husband Adron was a good man, but Vera knew that wouldn't save him from the penalty of his sins. Through the years she kept praying for her beloved mate and had others praying, too. She would get discouraged sometimes about going to church alone and not being able to talk about the things of the Lord with her husband; but she just kept looking to the Lord.

"Oh, Lord, if only Adron could be saved during my lifetime!" she would cry. "If it could please You just to give us one day together to enjoy spiritual fellowship!"

Vera also knew the type of life she led before her husband was of vital importance, as First Peter 3:1 says: "Wives, in the same way be submissive to your husbands so that if any of them do not believe the word, they may be won over without talk by the behavior of their wives."

"Give me a sweetness, Lord, in the way I live with my husband," Vera prayed many times, "that he might see Christ in me. Give me self-control not to answer back and wisdom to live with him as a good Christian wife should."

"The Lord gave me both wisdom and patience," Vera told me. "I knew they had to come from Him, for in my flesh I wouldn't have had them."

That Saturday 24 years after Vera first started praying and believing God for the salvation of her husband, they drove along in the car listening to a George Beverly Shea tape. As he sang "The King is Coming," Aldron suddenly cried to Vera, "Pull over to the side of the road!"

"What's the matter? Are you sick, Adron?" Vera asked in alarm. He had a thunder-struck look on his face.

"No, I'm not sick," he blurted out. "I've just got to be saved. Pray for me!"

Vera pulled to the side of the road. She could hardly believe her ears. That was what she had wanted to hear for so many years! A lump filled her throat. Adron was crying.

Vera prayed and then turned to her husband and explained to him how he could become a child of God. She ended by saying, " 'Whosoever shall call upon the name of the Lord shall be saved.' Do you want to do that right now?"

Adron nodded and began to pray. The words tumbled out as he called upon the Lord to save him for Jesus' sake. The happy couple just sat there by the side of the road crying together for joy.

A short while later, as they went on their way, Adron told his wife that as George Beverly Shea had sung about belonging to the King, he knew he didn't. He had realized then he wasn't ready for the King's coming; he was lost and on his way to hell. Then he had had the strange, awful feeling that he was going to die right then if he didn't do something.

Adron could hardly wait to get home to call various friends and tell them the good news. He has been going to church ever since with his wife, and they now have the sweet fellowship in Christ she had always longed for.

WHOLE FAMILIES CAN BE SAVED

After I turned my life over to the Lord at the age of 24, I immediately had a concern for my husband especially. I knew he definitely did not believe in Jesus Christ as his Savior. He had often said he thought Jesus was a great teacher, but just a good man. He had often scoffed at the Bible, and his arguments had undermined my childhood faith. He didn't believe the story of Adam and Eve was true or that Jesus had been born of a virgin. He was an evolutionist.

I was just a babe in Christ, but I knew how the Lord had worked in my life to draw me to Himself. I began to pray for my husband. It had always been impossible for me to win an argument with that half-Irishman, and really it seemed unlikely that he would ever come to Jesus. I decided subtlety was my best course.

When we lived in Perth Amboy, New Jersey, I became the paid organist at a Hungarian Lutheran church where the gospel was preached. "It really doesn't look right if the organist's husband doesn't come," I said to Al. So he came to church with me and heard the gospel.

After we moved from there to Roselle Park, New Jersey, I began turning on religious radio and television programs; and Al listened and looked with me. One Sunday a program offered a free Bible course. "I'm going to find out what that Bible is all about," Al declared. He sent for the course and started doing the lessons.

One night, as he poured over the Bible, he came to a question in the course: "Have you ever received Jesus Christ as your personal Savior?" He paused and looked at the next question. "Would you like to do it right now?" He wrote down "Yes" and bowed his head and asked Christ to be his Savior.

Overnight Al's views about the Bible and Christ were changed. Suddenly he believed the Bible from cover to cover: Adam and Eve; Jonah and the big fish; Jesus, the Son of God and the virgin Mary. In answer to prayer, the Lord led us to a Bible-believing church where we were baptized and grew in Him. Eventually God called Al to the ministry.

One Sunday when evangelist Larry McGill was

preaching at our church, Hydewood Park Baptist in North Plainfield, New Jersey, we brought my parents. We had been praying especially for my 51-year-old father, who had been reared a Roman Catholic, but did not know Christ personally. Dad walked the aisle that day and gave his heart to Christ. On the same day our six-year-old daughter, Gay, received Christ in Junior Church.

Dad and Mother started serving the Lord in a church near their home. Three years later God answered our prayers for my brother Gene and his wife, whose story of salvation I have already told. Thus my whole family came to know Christ as Savior.

GOD'S GRACE TO A GODLESS FAMILY

Lib Davis grew up in a non-Christian home with twelve brothers and sisters. When she was 27, she heard a radio preacher speak on hell. She knelt by the radio and gave her heart to Christ. She immediately began praying for her husband and other members of her family.

Lib's husband often gave her a terrible time when she went to church with their six children. But after she prayed and witnessed for several years, Roy also came to Christ and his life was transformed. Through his changed life Lib's sister Helen realized she could be saved, too. She gave her heart to Christ, stopped drinking, and began to attend church regularly.

Lib had an opportunity to witness to her sister, Olive, shortly before Olive died. In answer to Lib's prayers, God sent a Christian friend of Olive's to lead her to Christ just before she went to be with her new-found Lord. Olive's husband also was led to the Lord that week on the front steps of the hospital.

At Olive's funeral Lib witnessed to her oldest sister, Bertha, who was very receptive, for the Holy Spirit had prepared her heart. "I've been concerned about my soul," Bertha admitted. Lib showed Bertha God's way of salvation in her Bible and then invited her to receive Christ. With tears in her eyes Bertha said she would and knelt with Lib to pray.

One of Lib's brothers came to the Lord as a result of a tragedy. In a three-way family argument between himself, his wife, and his mother-in-law, a loaded gun had gone off and the bullet had hit the brother's wife, killing her. Lib's brother was sentenced to two years in the penitentiary as an accessory to a murder. When he got out, the Davises took him into their home for a while. They talked to him about the Lord and salvation, and he said he had thought a lot about becoming a Christian while he was in prison. Lib led him to Christ.

The Davises also led three of her other brothers to Christ. When they visited her brother Jim's home in Atlanta, Jim's entire family fell under conviction of the Holy Spirit and they all knelt with the Davises to receive the Lord as their Savior.

When women truly believe, all the members of

their family may be saved in time. If even one person in a family comes to know the Savior personally, through that person all the family can be reached for Christ, no matter how godless that family may be.

The Bible says, "So then faith cometh by hearing, and hearing by the word of God" (Rom. 10:17). Christ came to open the ears of the deaf, and help the blind to see. When women believe in Him, He will do that for those they love.

SOMETHING YOU CAN DO:

1. Read First Peter 3:1-15. Ask the Lord to reveal what He has for you in this passage.

2. If you know Christ as your Savior, have you been sharing the good news with your lost loved ones? Ask the Lord to lead you in the best possible way to do this. Back it up with prayer and faith.

3. For study and discussion:

(a) How can a person be led to Christ? (Memorize the "Romans Road": Romans 3:23, 6:23, 5:8, 10:9-10, 13. Other Scriptures: John 1:12, 3:16, 14:6, 20:31; Hebrews 9:27; 1 John 1:9; Revelation 3:20.)

(b) What Scriptures can be used to help someone who believes in salvation by works to see that a person is saved by faith in Christ alone? (See John 3;36, 5:24, 6:29, 11:25; Acts 16:31; Romans 3:23-28, 4:5, 5:1; Galatians 2:16, 21; Ephesians 2:8-9; Titus 3:4-7; Hebrews 9:28, 10:10.)

12

EXCITING ADVENTURES IN FAITH

I have been crucified with Christ and I no longer live, but Christ lives in me. The life I live in the body, I live by faith in the Son of God who loved me and gave himself for me.

Galatians 2:20 (NIV)

"I wish I could do something great for the Lord!" Have you ever said or thought that? But perhaps you have never ventured beyond that. Maybe you have young children in the home and you think that keeps you from serving the Lord. Or maybe you feel timid about venturing out for the Lord on some project you may feel He wants you to start.

While I was still nursing my younger daughter, Lori, the Lord let me know He wanted me to start a Vacation Bible School in the small church we attended. I didn't see how I could do it, and I argued a bit with the Lord. But He informed me that I could hold the school in August after Lori was weaned. So with the permission of the leaders of the church I trained a group of women and we held the school. Children came to know Jesus, the women were thrilled, and ever since then a VBS has been held in that church in Dallas.

My friend Bea Fishter became a Christian at the age of 36. Bea attended a weekly Bible study I held in my home. One day she said, "Muriel, I have been asked to help teach in Vacation Bible School, but I don't think I can do that. I feel too inexperienced. Someone else can do a better job, I'm sure!"

"Bea," I said, "can Jesus do it?"

"Why, of course!"

"Doesn't Jesus live in you? Can't He do it through you?"

Bea's eyes lit up. "Why, of course He can!"

Bea started going to the preparation meetings for the VBS, and she loved every minute of the VBS itself. She found that indeed Christ could do His work through her.

However, she forgot that several months later when she was asked to hold a Bible club for children in her home. "I can't do that, Muriel!" she exclaimed to me. "I don't know enough!"

"Can Jesus do it through you?"

Bea grinned sheepishly. "OK, OK," she answered. "You're right!"

Bea started going to the monthly training meetings held by Child Evangelism and began holding a Bible club in her home. Through the years countless boys and girls from her neighborhood came to know Jesus as their Savior. Some of them started attending our church regularly and their parents were reached for Christ.

Eventually Bea became the yearly superintendent of the VBS beginner department, as well as director of the junior church program. What made her so useful in God's service? She believed that Jesus could do anything working through her yielded soul and body.

LEANING ON THE LORD

I have found that Christ accomplishes the most through His people when they realize they have to lean the most on Him, believing Him for wisdom and enablement. When people feel self-sufficient, they may be able to do things well by themselves, but the power of the Holy Spirit may be missing from their work.

For years I have served the Lord playing the piano, organ, and accordian in churches; at missions, rest homes, county jails; for Sunday schools, VBS, and Bible clubs. Sometimes I have felt so sure of myself, I forgot to pray before playing. And sometimes my mind has gone blank or I have made a serious mistake in playing or singing.

The first time I played my accordian in public was a month after I got it, at the McAuley Mission in New York City. I guess you know I prayed hard before going up on that stage! The accordian was heavy and my knees knocked together as I played; but I knew the Lord helped me get through that piece!

By nature I am not a very bold person, although all the opportunities I have had to speak and play instruments in public have given me a feeling of ease in that department. Also, Jesus promised that when the Holy Spirit came, He would give His disciples boldness to witness for Him; and I know that any boldness I have had in that department just has had to come from the Holy Spirit! So I know from personal experience that the Holy Spirit gives even timid people the courage they need to pass out tracts and witness whenever they find opportunity.

During the early seventies God gave me a Shasta camper in an unusual way. It was for sale at a garage sale for $1,000. "If I can get that for $800 for you, will you buy it?" my father asked.

"Sure," I answered flippantly. Well, he got it for me for $800, so I bought it, with the help of some royalty money I had recently received. The Lord immediately impressed on me that He was the One who had led in all this, and I was to use that camper for His glory. I was to go out to camping parks to hold Bible clubs for boys and girls and lead them to Christ. I had held Bible clubs in homes for some years, but the idea of going out cold like that really scared me. Nevertheless, I knew in my heart it was what the Lord wanted me to do, so I made plans to do it with His help and guidance.

In June we went to a state park located on a

lake. I prayed for a good site as we traveled; the Lord gave us the best, most-centrally located site in the park.

Then my battle with the devil began. "What if no children come to the Bible club?" he suggested. "You're just wasting your time and getting all tensed up for nothing. Why don't you just relax and enjoy your few days of vacation like most good workers for the Lord do?"

"But the Lord gave me this trailer to use for Him, too," I argued back.

"And what if some children do come?" he countered. "What if after you present the gospel to them, their parents get angry and complain to the ranger?"

He almost had me to the point of giving up. After all, I had never heard of anyone else doing something precisely like this. Who was I to do it? Yet I knew God's hand was in it, so I just trusted the Lord and went ahead.

Sixteen children came running to the club. Twelve of them made decisions for Christ. That evening one girl thanked me profusely for having held the club. "I've been wanting to get saved and so has my brother," she said, "but Mama doesn't like the preacher at our church and she wouldn't let us go down the aisle when the invitation was given. Now I'm so glad we had a chance to ask Jesus into our hearts today!"

How glad I was that I hadn't backed out! I have been holding my camper Bible clubs every summer since then, and have had the joy of leading children and teenagers from all over the United States and Canada to the Lord.

AGE DOESN'T MATTER

After forty happy years of marriage, Myriam Faust's beloved husband went to be with the Lord. As she was seeking comfort from Him one day, she heard Him say, "Do not weep for yourself, but weep for the millions who have never heard of me."

Myriam began to pray earnestly that God would call young people to go forth into the fields "white unto harvest." One day while she was praying, God's answer came back, "You go, Myriam Faust!"

Myriam had received a letter asking if she would be willing to be the housemother for the children of missionaries at the Morrison Academy in Taiwan. As she prayed, she knew this was where God was leading her. At the age of 63 she took off for Taiwan, paying her own way.

"You must be out of your mind, Myriam Faust!" said one well-meaning friend before she left. But time has proved she was not out of her mind, but in faith following God's leading.

Myriam had held Bible clubs for boys and girls for years in the United States. After she assumed her new position at the Academy, she started giving the missionary children Scripture to memorize and told them many stories using her flannelboard and figures.

A heavy burden was laid on Myriam's heart for the multitudes of Chinese children she saw. She hired a pedicab driver who also served as a translator for her when she went out in her spare time to tell flannelgraph stories to the Chinese children in the area. Before long, Boya Yang, her translator, became enthusiastic about reaching boys and girls, teenagers and adults for Christ, too. He would bring his clarinet and walk through the villages playing it, drawing large crowds of children, young people, and adults to where Myriam had her board set up.

Eventually Myriam and her young co-worker visited villages all over Taiwan, including a city where no missionary had ever come before. Many Taiwanese have come to know Christ as their personal Savior through Myriam and Boya, whom she adopted as her son. Age and even language are no barriers to God accomplishing great things through a woman who truly believes.

CIRCUMSTANCES DON'T MATTER

Maxine May of Castle Rock, Washington, started working with a group of women to influence people for Christ through Bible correspondence courses put out by The Mailbox Club of Valdosta, Georgia. When the young woman who had started the work was planning to move to Alaska, someone had to take over the leadership. The Lord told Maxine she was the one.

"Oh, Lord," she said, "I have no training as a secretary or bookkeeper. Until we get our new home built, we have to live in this trailer. Where would I put all that material?"

But Maxine finally gave in to the call of the Lord. She trusted He would work out all the details since this was what He wanted her to do. And He did. He supplied all the wisdom and knowledge Maxine needed during the months and years ahead. Yes, the trailer was filled with boxes of material; but Maxine was happy knowing she was in the Lord's will.

Under Maxine's direction the work grew until they had 36 Christians of all ages serving as teachers for more than 1300 children, teenagers, and adults in seven states. Through her influence several other such Mailbox Clubs were started in other areas. Hundreds of people have come to know Christ as their Savior and have grown in grace and knowledge of the Lord and His Word. A number of older and physically-handicapped women, as well as mothers with little children, are able to serve the Lord in this good work which they can do at home.

Thanks to one woman who believed God, this Mailbox Club is one of the largest of the six hundred such clubs that now engage in this mission outreach.

PROFESSIONALISM DOESN'T MATTER

When Jesus chose His disciples, He didn't take them from among the scribes and Pharisees. For the most part they were simple, barely educated lay people. He used a woman who had been immoral as the first witness to the Samaritans. He used a woman out of whom He had cast seven demons as the first witness to His resurrection. They were't great preachers. They were just women who believed.

Grace Rainey wasn't a great preacher or evangelist. Certainly she wasn't a professional religious leader. She was just a counselor for a call-in program on the Christian television station in Greenville, South Carolina. She was also the owner of a five-and-ten-cent store. But that hardly qualified her for the thing God seemed to lay on her heart.

Grace had a vision of many, many people before her. But she had the impression that they couldn't see her. For three weeks she puzzled over that, feeling the Lord was trying to tell her something. As she prayed, one day the thought came to her of a fifteen-minute radio program designed for shut-ins or for people who didn't go to church.

Why that's absurd! she thought. *With so many professional people who preach on the air on Sunday, surely God wouldn't lead a 48-year-old laywoman to do it!* But He did. He opened the way as soon as Grace laid down her objections and believed.

Just before Grace phoned a local station, the manager had received a call canceling a 15-minute program on Sunday mornings. Grace got the 15 minutes on radio for $16 a week; she would be able to tape it on a weekday. That night the Lord gave her the name for the program: "Tidings of Hope." He also gave her the theme for the first program, a theme that was so fresh in her own experience: when you are willing to follow the Lord all the way, He will lead you in paths you would never dream you would walk.

Grace varied her programs. Sometimes she did the talking, sometimes she interviewed, and at other times she invited someone else to speak or sing. She rejoiced as people called to tell her how they had accepted Christ as their Savior as a result of her program, and when others called to tell her how the program had changed their lives and outlooks and had blessed them. Because she believed, this woman of God has been greatly used to His glory.

WHAT DOES MATTER

What does matter is a believing and willing heart. I have found in my own experience that as I have stepped out in faith to do whatever the Lord has led me to do, He has opened one door after another to service. It is an exciting adventure being in the Lord's employ. Not only does He give you the job, but He gives you the power, talent, wisdom, and ability to do it.

I don't think of myself as anything special. God just uses me because I'm willing and believing. It was the same way with these other women whose stories I have told. It can be the same way with you.

SOMETHING YOU CAN DO:

1. Read Hebrews 11. Ask the Lord what He has for you in this Scripture.

2. The Lord has special assignments for every one of His children. He gives every one of us one or more talents to use for His glory. Ask the Lord to give you a believing and willing heart, and to show you what He wants you to do. It may not be something unusual; but if you step out in faith and obey Him, you will have great joy.

3. For study or discussion:

(a) What talents or abilities does God give His people with which to serve Him? (See Exodus 15:20-26, 31:1-6; Judges 4:4-9; 1 Samuel 16:16, 23; 1 Chronicles 25:6-7; Acts 9:36-39; Romans 12:4-8; 1 Corinthians 12:4-11, 28.)

(b) What are some ways in which we all should serve the Lord? (See Psalms 89:1, 96:2-9; Daniel 12:3; Matthew 5:13-16; Acts 1:8; Romans 1:16; 10:9; Colossians 3:16.)

13

HOW TO BELIEVE

*Now faith is being sure of what we hope for and
certain of what we do not see*

Hebrews 11:1, (NIV)

Would you like to have the kind of faith that
would release the power of God on your behalf and
those you love? You can, you know, if you follow
certain principles set forth in God's Word. Let me
share those principles with you.

BE GOD'S CHILD

To become God's child a person has to come to
Him like a little child in faith and humility. That is
why it was so hard for those proud people, the
Pharisees, to accept Christ. They were so wise in
their own conceits, so intelligent, so great in their
own esteem! Many people like that today will
never come to know the Lord, for they will never
humble themselves.

Jesus said, "I tell you the truth, unless you

change and become like little children, you will never enter the kingdom of heaven" (Matt. 18:3).

What is a little child like? His conscience is sensitive; he knows when he has done wrong. I have dealt with many children in my child evangelism work and have led many to Christ. Through their tender consciences the Holy Spirit has readily convicted them that they have done wrong and they need Jesus. The Bible says, "For all have sinned and come short of the glory of God" (Rom. 3:23). Before we see our need for the Savior, we must see our need to be saved because of our sinfulness.

A little child readily believes what he is told. He readily believes everything about Jesus. A little three-year-old I know pointed to a picture of Jesus one day and exclaimed, "That is God—that is *my* God!"

So we must believe and accept what John 3:16 says, "For God so loved the world that he gave his only begotten Son, that whosoever believeth in him should not perish but have everlasting life." Eugenia Price and many others have been born again because they believed what that verse says.

I have met people who seemed to think salvation is so complicated. You've got to do this; you've got to do that; you can't be saved until you're well-nigh perfect. That may be one reason why Charlotte Elliott's invitation song, "Just As I Am," is so effective. It knocks down all the false ideas about salvation, and so beautifully brings out the fact that we are saved by faith alone, plus nothing.

Here is the gospel: We are lost sinners. God loved us so much He sent His Son, Jesus Christ, to die on the cross to pay the penalty for our sins so that we could be forgiven and receive eternal life. God raised Christ from the grave for our justification. Jesus Christ is alive; He lives in the hearts of His people through His Spirit; He intercedes for them in heaven; He is coming back to earth, perhaps any day now, to receive His own (1 Cor. 15:1-4; John 14:3).

If you are not sure that you are a child of God that you have ever received Christ as your Savior, why not pray the words of "Just As I Am":

Just as I am, without one plea,
But that Thy blood was shed for me,
And that Thou bidd'st me come to Thee,
O Lamb of God, I come! I come!

Just as I am, though tossed about,
With many a conflict, many a doubt,
Fightings and fears within, without,
O Lamb of God, I come! I come!

Just as I am—Thou wilt receive,
Wilt welcome, pardon, cleanse, relieve,
Because Thy promise I believe,
O Lamb of God, I come! I come!

HEAR GOD'S WORD

Romans 10:17 says, "So then faith cometh by hearing, and hearing by the Word of God." Reading, hearing, and memorizing God's Word plants faith in our hearts and strengthens it. That is why it is so important for a Christian to faithfully attend a Bible-believing church where he is fed the Word of

God in Sunday school, worship services, and prayer meeting.

You can become a person of great faith, and thus one whose prayers are answered, by spending time in God's Word every day, allowing it to speak to your heart. God's Word reminds us in so many places of how God loves us, cares for us, and will help us in every problem. As we are reminded day by day, we grow in faith. A Christian doesn't become a spiritual giant overnight; she has to grow into it (1 Pet 2:2; 2 Pet. 3:18).

One who really *hears* God's Word is one who obeys it. God says, "Only believe" (Luke 8:50) . . . "Trust in the Lord with all thine heart" (Prov. 3:5) . . . "Be anxious about nothing" (Phil. 4:6) . . . "Rest in the Lord and wait patiently for him" (Ps. 37:7). Do you see how our faith is increased if we in obedience make instructions like these a part of our way of life?

When I was helping to work my husband's way through Bible college, I had a job near enough to home that I could walk to work. After my husband and daughter left for school, I had a few minutes in which I could read a chapter of God's Word and talk to Him. Every morning I selected two verses out of that chapter to memorize as I walked to work. Each day I rehearsed what I had already learned. I hid more than 300 verses from God's Word in my heart that way. Memorizing God's Word, hiding it in your heart, is a wonderful way to increase your faith! For thus God's Word really becomes a part of you.

PRESENT YOUR BODY

Romans 12:1-2 says, "I beseech you therefore, brethren, by the mercies of God, that ye present your bodies a living sacrifice, holy, acceptable unto God, which is your reasonable service. And be not conformed to this world; but be ye transformed by the renewing of your mind, that ye may prove what is that good, and acceptable, and perfect, will of God."

This plea is made to Christians who have already given their hearts to the Lord. Now there is something more they must give: their bodies a living sacrifice. What exactly does this mean? It means you are turning your body over to the Lord *to live in it*. Yes, He lives in your heart. But if He has your whole body, He will use and guide those hands and feet as if they were His own, as if He Himself were walking this earth in your body. Isn't that exciting?

God teld feet as if they were His own, as if He Himself were walking this earth in your body. Isn't that exciting?

God tells us to be filled with the Spirit. In order for us to be filled with the Holy Spirit, we must lay our bodies, our will, our lives, our intellect, everything, on the altar. Self must go so that the Spirit may reign in our hearts and lives. We must be willing for the Lord to take over. We must die daily to self so that the Spirit may continue to fill us, so that the living water Christ promised will continue to flow out from us to others.

Have you ever wondered why it is some Christian seems to have a face like an angel? And you think, *I can see Jesus in her.* That is who you are seeing. Most certainly that is a person who has presented her body a living sacrifice; Jesus is walking the earth in her; His Spirit is filling her with the fruit of love, peace, and joy.

If you get to know that woman, you will find she is a woman of great faith. She is a woman to whom people bring their problems and prayer requests because they know her prayers get answered. Why? Because she believes.

A woman filled with the Spirit doesn't think overmuch of herself. The closer you walk with your Lord, the more humble you feel. You don't belittle yourself, for you are a child of God, a princess! Yet such a woman doesn't feel proud; she does feel exceedingly blessed and rich, for she is a vessel filled and run by Jesus.

Any woman can be that. You can be that.

WALK AND TALK WITH GOD

The Bible says, "Pray without ceasing" (1 Thess. 5:17). How many times have we sung, "And I walked with Him, and I talked with Him, and He tells me I am His own . . ."? But do we ever stop to think, Have *I* experienced *that*?

We are busy people today, rushing here and there, doing this and that. But even if we have a lot to do, there are many times during the day when we can walk and talk with God and experience His presence and listen to His voice. Yes, LISTEN TO

HIS VOICE. Certainly if Satan can talk to people and assail them with temptations (James 4:7), God—who lives in our hearts—can talk to us. The trouble is, most of us are so busy and so surrounded with noise and have so little time to stop to listen to God, that we never hear His tender voice.

Christians can quench the Spirit by not listening to Him when He tries to tell them something (1 Thess. 5:19). They can grieve the Spirit by their unloving and un-Christian ways (Eph. 4:30-31). No wonder so many professing Christians don't know what it is to walk and talk with the Lord!

I enjoy talking with the Lord all the time. He is the first one I think of when I awake in the morning. I start my day talking with Him, praying to Him, telling Him I love Him, and thanking Him for various blessings. During the day I bring various petitions for others to Him as they come to my mind. When I read letters from various missions, I pray for their requests right then. When someone calls me about a need or problem, we talk to the Lord about it while we're still on the phone. Whenever I'm driving the car, I find it's a wonderful time to talk with the Lord. One can pray for a lot of people and needs at such a time as that.

When I've misplaced or lost something, I ask the Lord to lead me to where it is or put it in my mind where to look. After all, He knows everything, right? So He helps me find it. When something goes wrong with my typewriter or car, I ask the Lord to guide me as to what to do. He never fails! Sometimes He helps me fix the thing myself; other times He leads me to the right mechanic or store.

I don't become discouraged when my prayers are not answered. God knows what He wants to do. He has His own timetable. Also, sometimes when I start to pray for something—as I prayed for my father's healing from cancer when it was first discovered—the Lord restrains me and lays on my heart just to pray that His will will be done. It was His will to take my father home. Dad was 79 years old, and he had other physical problems associated with old age. God knows what is best. He will lay on our hearts what to pray for.

As we daily or weekly see answers to prayers in little and big things, our faith is increased; we become women who truly believe. The more we believe, the more our prayers are answered.

PRAISE AND THANKSGIVING

The Bible says, "Do not be anxious about anything, but in everything, by prayer and petition, with thanksgiving, present your requests to God" (Phil. 4:6, NIV). That sentence is made complex by the addition of the words "with thanksgiving," but those words are vital to that excellent advice from God.

Think of it now: while you are on your knees bringing all your problems to the Lord, you stop and begin thanking Him for all He has done for you in the past, all the answers to prayer you have already had. What does that do?

First of all, it shows the Lord you really appreciate what He has done for you already, the answers to prayer He has given. When you do something nice for someone, don't you like that person to express his appreciation for it?

Sometimes the Lord answers a prayer for me and I will forget to thank Him right away. Then it will come to me a day or two later: *Why, the Lord answered my prayer! Praise the Lord!* "Thank You, Jesus!" And I have the feeling in my heart that perhaps one reason He does answer our prayers is that we appreciate what He already has done for us. Do we enjoy doing things for ungrateful people? Not usually!

If when you are bringing your requests to God, you can think of nothing else He has done for you but save your soul and give you eternal life and adopt you as His daughter—what greater thing could you thank Him for? Your circumstances may be miserable on this earth, but you have a glorious future in Heaven.

Another reason it is important to bring your requests with thanksgiving is that it reminds *you* of how the Lord has helped you in the past, of all He has already done for you. We are forgetful creatures. We tend to get our eyes so glued on our present woes that they overwhelm us. It clean escapes our minds how powerful our God is, how much He loves us, how much He can do for us. But as we kneel there recounting His past blessings and answers to prayer, faith springs in our hearts anew.

When we ask God for anything, we must have faith in order to receive it (James 1:5-7). The Bible says, "But without faith it is impossible to please him; for he that cometh to God must believe that he is, and that he is a rewarder of them that diligently seek him" (Heb. 11:6). We must believe!

Finally, let us learn how to praise the Lord. When we are filled with His Spirit, praising the Lord comes naturally. But when we are young in the Lord, there are up and down periods. Also, no matter how long we are with the Lord, we have times of testing, times of trial. These times are necessary; for as the winds strengthen trees, so such times will make us strong in the Lord. They increase our faith. We learn to sing songs in the night.

It is easy to praise the Lord when we are up on Cloud Nine, when we are happy. It is not so easy when we're down in the slough of despond or struggling through the valley of the shadow of death. So here is how you can increase your spirit of praise at such times: read the Book of Psalms. My favorites are Psalms 23, 24, 37, 42, 50, 51, 89, 95, 103, and 139. Praising and thanking the Lord helps to lift us out of depression. Notice how many psalms start with the sound of despair and defeat and end with the note of triumph!

Jesus said, "If ye abide in me, and my words abide in you, ye shall ask what ye will, and it shall be done unto you" (John 15:7). So if we would be women who believe, let us abide in our Lord Jesus. Let us allow His Spirit to fill us, to guide us, to use us to His glory. The end result of true faith in the Lord is love, peace, joy, goodness, confidence, and the "abundant life" Christ promised His followers.

If every woman who reads this book becomes such a woman who believes, we can—as it says of Christians in Acts 17:6—turn this world upside down for our Lord Jesus Christ!